Alphabet Noise

poems by

Thomas Townsley

Alphabet Noise Copyright © 2025 by Thomas Townsley

ISBN: 978-1-7339321-5-8

All rights reserved. Printed in the United States of America.

No part of this book may be used or reproduced in any manner whatsoever without written permission from the author or copyright holder, except in the case of brief quotations embodied in critical articles or reviews.

First Edition
First Printing

The text of this book is set in Optima and Big Caslon.

Book and Cover Design by William Welch.

Doubly Mad Books
Utica, New York

Doubly Mad Books is affiliated with *Doubly Mad: Utica's Independent Journal of Arts and Ideas*, both operated by The Other Side of Utica, Inc., a 501(c)(3) organization located at 2011 Genesee St., Utica, NY, 13501.

For more information, visit:

theothersideutica.org
doublymad.org

Table of Contents

The Mune Monologues	1
The Arena	10
Effulgence at Three O'Clock	15
Dopic	19
Oof!	22
Famous Last Words	28
Carnal Acoustics	49
Time Curve Postlude	58
Furthermore	60
Tapioca Verdigris	63
Stop Charging Us Money To Watch You Sleep	66

Acknowledgments

About the Author

ALPHABET NOISE

The Mune Monologues

"If it were spelled "mune" it would not cause madness." —Jack Spicer

1

At night I whisper to Lazarus. I hum along as the new moon practices its dirges. The trick is to cry anodyne tears and accept defeat as colorlessly as possible. "All roses are faux roses"—let that be your creed. What kind of darkness comes with handlebars? Who clings to a dream's kite tail? These are the questions for which questioning was invented by pre-Orphic well diggers in the Herbaceous Era. Please direct all queries to the Yes Man.

The truth is, I've been carrying your dark groceries for too long. Yet even now, I'd like to watch you chewing gristle. I'd place my thumb *just* so. I'd let you stand naked in the lawn sprinkler, throwing croutons at magpies, knowing full well that thirty-seven kinds of rain couldn't wet you. Still, my Jacobite longing will not be assuaged. Like the octopus outside my vestibule, it has three hearts, only one of which is incapable of carrying a tune. So be thankful German engineering only goes so far.

Be thankful, too, that those Latin cognates died in your throat like rats in a rain barrel—and remember, that leper in chiffon could be your doppelganger's uncle bringing corn pies home from the fair. I still recall how the scent of hermeneutical varnish permeated the noumena, as Mother suspended six kinds of meat in aspic. That's how we celebrated Lent in the Seventies. Such grim determination: no one would out-Leviticus *our* lunchboxes! The world's fontanelle had yet to close. Blue candles had yet to be invented; maybe they never would be; it was none of my business, really. I was crouched behind an obsidian mountain, watching your shadow draw zeros and ones on pale parchment. Your incognito lips reminded me: some veils are meant to have zippers; some buttons are born to bleed. But why must your whispered "no's" constantly lave my cochlea, leaving a residue of moon aloe? Thanks to you, my scotopic vision is 20-20. Thanks to you, the night is drained of metaphors—I watch them recede with their twirling parasols and humming stigmata into someone else's thought experiment.

Meanwhile, the dog star rages. My Merkel's discs stand at rapt attention. Shall we dine al fresco? This bear trap once belonged to Friedrich Hegel; now it belongs to the bear. Some say that the mythological imagination is in remission; I say that the idee fixe is on vacation. Gestalt theory teaches us that some "top-down processing" is inevitable, so help yourself to these faux roses—and please be patient! We are working toward a more scientific alphabet.

Last Tuesday, the Yes Man manifested at our front door, carrying a suitcase full of lip balm. He said, "I sense a vague dissatisfaction gnawing at our utterances. Perhaps we should recite some litanies to reduce the swelling. But would doing so cure the moon itch plaguing us all?" By this time, he'd gotten a foot inside the door and begun to open his suitcase. "This lip balm is laced with calming pheromones—it's our only hope! Say, is that aspic I smell?" Mother smiled. She took him by the hand. Together, they went upstairs, while Father mounted another jackalope head to the wall.

2

I fell through my own trap door. Or perhaps I was pushed. Was it you? Your three-pronged lance put me in a subjunctive mood; the feverish glare of your Byzantine breastplate roused my amygdala from its starfish dreams. O sleep tumescent! Why attach so much consciousness to desire? The elevator operator with the handlebar mustache cannot guess your middle name; I caught you writing crib notes in invisible ink; now a white lynx prowls your periphery, guarding what's left of your chastity; I stare until I'm snow-blind, until everything seems imaginary, including me.

And thus, alone in my pensive citadel, I ask myself: when the wallpaper of appearances is stripped away, will the solipsistic rose hum with a clearer flame? Will the moon expectorate, and will you, sugar-newt, fall in love with shadows? If so, I'll order a cheese omelet and arrange my keyhole collection in a glass display case formerly reserved for emblems of melancholy; then we can cancel our dentist appointments, and our erogenous zones will form perfect circles. At this point, I assume, all will be revealed, and we'll know the consequences of this and that, and everything will blossom in an effulgence of Monday rain, causing our rhizomes to sparkle like new-fallen sequins beneath the interrogator's floodlight while the angry mimes surrounding us melt away, leaving us free to gaze at our invisible wounds in mute appreciation. Then will your penchants bristle with declivities, as an engorged moon rises above the gun shop—the one that doubles as a massage parlor, or so I'm told.

"It's true," says the Yes Man, emerging from behind the viburnum and brandishing a valise full of eiderdown. "Just the other day, a convivial masseuse asked me if I wanted to buy ammunition. His ingratiating tone bore its own distinct message, separate from that of his 'implied narrative.' Nevertheless, his technique was excellent; under his maestro's touch, my chakras were completely exfoliated. Would you like me to demonstrate?"

"That won't be necessary," I tell him.

At this precise moment, Mother steps out of the kitchen, bearing a floral-patterned saucière. "Does this gravy look demoralized?" she asks.

Naturally, I refuse to look. Instead, I mount the porch swing, my thoughts of you already caramelized by flute-wielding hormones. Even now, I can feel something oblique besetting us—all the signs are here, ripe for misreading.

Is this where I recall the slow rain of orchids as we groped beneath the trellis? Is this where I summon the memory of your flammable hips, your calcimine eyes with their bus terminal gaze, your emotional onion snows and the black ice of your affection, your eschatological smile with bits of God stuck between your teeth, your scent of confused lilies, your throat from which broken promises scuttle like mice, your grenadine sympathies and secret doorbells, your brittle manifestos, your titanium tears, your spiritual subwoofer, your poison honeysuckle kisses, your barbed-wire-and-cotton-candy voice with its ravenous plentitude of humdingers and sparkling bon mots, your deflective puppetry, your imaginary lapis lazuli-studded chastity belt and lugubrious horsehair cushions, your metaphysical salt mines and your hypnagogic hallucinations, your taste of marabou and that cobra trance you mistake for love, your pyrite sensibilities in financial matters, your World Fair torso and Teflon lips, your direct plumb-line to Nostradamus, your petroleum jelly heart and xylophone kneecaps and pardon-me-can-you-direct-me-to-the-nearest-monastery thighs?

The loud "Ahem!" of Father clearing his throat interrupts my revery. He squats beside me, removes his fleshing blade from its sheath, and begins to polish it, using one of Mother's nylon stockings. "Remember when summer was like a fat girl, whispering dirty secrets?" he says. "I wish we could have those days again."

3

Look out! That xylophone is leaking butane, and this kaleidoscope's rash may be contagious! What lovely pincers! Do not mistake me for one with a didactic mission just because I'm waving to you from this jetty. Keep tossing your desire from a red steeple if you think it helps. Were you born with those zippers? I suggest that we smoke until dawn, or at least until the screaming vexations molt into angels with salt on their tails—which reminds me: how many types of angels have you seen? Have you seen the translucent ones with accordions for hearts who sing high Eb's above the rooftops, tormenting neighborhood dogs into a frenzy of howling? Or the ones with hourglasses for eyes whose songs compel men to think allegorically and dream of keys to non-existent maps? How about the ones with accidents for hands who hover over dead men's houses, pointing at the moon—whose mouths form perfect circles from which only radio static can be heard?

The most terrifying angel was one I heard but never saw. One morning when I was in the throes of adolescence, while walking on a beach in Sea Isle City, I came upon a large whelk shell in the swash zone, a plaything of the waves, or so it seemed. Intact whelk shells were a rare find in such a populous area, so, congratulating myself on my luck, I picked it up and held it to my ear, as children do, expecting to "hear the sea." Instead, a small, inhuman voice, like sculpted white noise, spiraled up from deep within the pink labyrinth and slithered into my ear, whispering "It is only pain. It is only pain. It is only pain." I did not know exactly what it meant, but I felt plate tectonics within me shift, and since then, I've suffered from alternating bouts of lust and spiritual malaise, characterized by waking dream incursions and involuntary troping—a sort of linguo-ontological Tourette's. The symptoms are especially acute at night, when I sometimes experience waves of synesthesia that translate moonlight into Gesualdo madrigals or cricket song into psoriasis. That disembodied Angel of the Whelk Shell has made its home in my head ever since, an itch, a thorn, a parasite, that can seemingly manifest at will, broadcasting its tribulations on any number of frequencies. Sometimes it even speaks in *your* voice, my little *ding an sich*.

I know others have heard it, too. Last night, in my favorite tavern, Willy, the new bartender, was polishing shot glasses when, apropos of nothing, he began to weep. "A vaster world awaits a place in our perception, awaits our grasp," he sobbed. Then his voice rose, causing the palimpsest of conversations around us to cease. Customers looked up from their drinks and stared like dogs detecting a far-off whistle. "Metaphysics is the abandonment of Being!" Willy cried, and then, perhaps more ominously, "This pilsner is on the house!" That broke the tension. All the customers applauded, and Willy forced an uncertain smile, too, as if in acknowledgment. But I knew. And as the drinking resumed, I glanced outside the plate glass window and saw seven gray angels with wings of supernal Velcro, flying in trapezoidal patterns above the parking lot, carrying abacuses instead of lyres and singing of love using imaginary numbers in place of words.

4

I forget the acronym for my disorder. Someone demagnetized the goulash, and now the leukocytes sing beautifully. What accounts for my aesthetic sanctimony? With beveled sunlight accosting our bathos, it's no wonder we felt little slices of the past returning to haunt us, trailing wilted poinsettias in their wake.

Was this the "sincerity" for which we scoured the source texts?

It's true. I'm twice the man today I will be tomorrow—maybe more—but to say "nothing happened" in my life would be an understatement, though accurate—and therein lies a theorem. Before I try to set it down, however, may I suggest we keep these poinsettia bracts in a vase? For as Wikipedia foretold, some bracts are more colorful than the "true flower"—and that's the case here, wouldn't you agree? So bring me my syllabus at once, and let's all take notes before the ospreys swoop down, rending the pastel breeze in twain with farcical cries and paper streamers.

Having once laid claim to an education, I no longer need to ask, "Who damasked these nasturtiums?"

Instead, I ask, "Must this gloaming forever be our lot?"

Do you see the difference?

According to the syllabus, today's class is about solar wind—and the way the earth's magnetic shield protects us from its radiation, which longs to kill us. "You could say the shield is a mark of God's providence," says the professor, "though of course, God made the radiation, too, didn't He? In any case, to understand this phenomenon correctly, we must first remember: a mark of Providence is not the same as a sign. Let's turn to Saussure . . ."

After that, things get rather technical.

Now, as I watch the moonlight paint my humming pillow blue, here is what I know: somewhere in what old-timers still call "the dark," a near-sighted glazier whistles "Aura Lee" in his sleep. Is it a harbinger of things to come, or just a song his mother used to sing? The syllabus doesn't say.

Did you know that nasturtiums are edible? Did you know that they produce an airborne chemical that repels aphids, beetles, and squash bugs? Did you know that they serve as symbols for "patriotism, love, loyalty, strength, and purity"? Not even faux roses take on that much freight!

Yet as an educated man, I must ask, "Who gets to say what 'patriotism, love, loyalty, strength, and purity' mean? Is it you, little *Zaubermaus*? Also—what's a squash bug?"

For the educated man, such questioning is a way of life:

Which hem-length goes best with flat ontologies?

How many heads of pins would support Friedrich Hegel dancing a jig?

Who took Occam's razor to Anselm's proof?

I have learned to read carefully, combing every text for landmines of possible symbols, such as eternal flames, sacred springs, bird bones arrayed on silver plates, peacock tails with blinking eyes, serpents whispering Latin aphorisms to gum-cracking altar boys, hag-mist, moon-glitter, thorn juice and cross varnish, The Six Dancing Chromosomes of Vaudeville, the morse code of quasars, melancholy hypotenuses, sirens who keep albatrosses as emotional support animals, deontological swastikas, wise-talking carp and lisping nightingales, Nietzsche-dust, a forgotten saint's navel lint that's said to cure scalp-itch, and postmodern seraphim who quote Wittgenstein while hovering over bowling alleys.

Nights, I whisper secrets into sinkholes.

Cloaked women with clock mechanisms for eyes want to know: "Can you hear the asps, circling the well?"

When the moon gets something caught between its teeth, why do I assume it's my "learning objectives"?

Remember how the village thespians performed morality plays from the back of a white truck?

Remember the cardboard props, the bowls of steaming millet, the razor wire—or the way Jack-in-the-box music seemed to emanate from your thalamus?

In a yellow room, the turnstile operator picks up radio signals in his metal skull plate. "I think they're playing our song," he says.

As night falls, Mother serves prosthetic bread to her new suitor.

I'm installing doorbells on every mirror in the house. Soon the incessant ringing will drive the villagers mad.

And in our bedroom, as always, the burning carousel spins round and round.

5

What roses remain have nothing left to do. And that sickle moon—better look it up in Cirlot's *Book of Symbols* before it's too late. (Who am I kidding? It's already too late. Already these monologues subsume memory, the way "capitalism absorbs its own critique.")

Wait, there's more! These chitinous shells of words taste like after-dinner mints—quite unlike the melodious taste of persimmons, which overwhelms the poor little drawbridge operator whose raincoat is lost. Poets, why do you devote massive expenditures of energy in service to tongue depressors? Can't you see how the allegorical figure of Venery, riding a unicycle, careens toward night eternal? Do you not feel the urgency? *Is anyone out there?*

They say nothing matters but the quality of the affection, which management in its wisdom has decided to "phase in" gradually. And therefore, awash in hermeneutical chem trails, the horizon itself shimmers, oozing mirages from which A Stranger will emerge—the one we've been waiting for, undoubtedly, moist with billowy foam and bloated with promises, the nature of which we have yet to surmise.

Did I tell you my Wednesday focus group once opined that poetry was the vestigial remains of an Ur-language? Then we waited for the winter wind to transform the trestle bridge on which we stood into an aeolian harp, but it was a "no go."

Afterwards, Louise passed around Ritz crackers with some kind of olive spread.

What I remember most about those days was how you tried to give my poem mouth-to-mouth resuscitation. You wanted to "cure it" of its ills. I think you still do. Or maybe it's me you're hoping to cure. You've been giving us chemo for weeks now, and still, you say my poem "doesn't mean anything,"—or rather, it has more meanings than a single body should bear, like a lumpy old dog that doesn't knows it's ugly. I sit holding my poem's hand and watch you move from bed to bed in your crisp white coat, inserting your long needles and making notes on your chart, while outside the window you never see, three-headed cherubs hover above the medical waste bins, tossing syringes down on hare-lipped fauns who varnish my hurdy-gurdies in exchange for menthol cigarettes and pocket lint.

6

Darker now. All those sleepovers on minted sheets, transformed by the pickle-brine of memory—how I age! My face in the mirror is raw pork. A thousand ping-pong balls must drop on this linoleum floor immediately, or else I won't be responsible for your haircut. As expected, a singing cobra slithers in via the narthex. "Melancholy Baby," is it? I feel the thrill and disappointment of having met you. It's true, I've had to rehearse what comes "naturally" to others, though "naturally" is a problematic term ever since Nixon left office. Most sandwiches prove anti-climactic, don't you think? I blame it on "committee work" and all those "breakout sessions," on "caring administrators" who outnumber us six to one, on pumice smiles and moon lard gumming up the mainsail's unholy riggings, like eviscerated doilies on All Hallows Eve.

Ah, February! The scent of plaster of Paris, sticky crewcuts! Remember to turn off the blender when you're through. Lately my laptop has been whispering to me—sweet somethings, imminent rain, conjugal visits, leprosy. This cochineal dwarfs my imagination, sleepyhead.

Darker now. Balloon animals infiltrate the well-worn similes. More liverwurst? Yes Man, Yes Man, why won't you put down your pitch pipe? What gesture or jester seems called for? O sacred gene pool, why must you tie me to the tracks? Management declares the reset button off limits. How I age! How I age! A bubble bath to slake my medulla! "As long as there is straining toward style, there is versification" says Mallarme. The Yes Man practices ragas before imaginary magpies. A thousand yo-yos descend at once. Behind the veil—more zinc! Did you remember to shut off the blender? What's the plural of "trapeze"?

Someone is spitting up jigsaw puzzle pieces. Can't you see I'm blackberrying? A macaw challenges me to a journalism contest but makes me promise not to say "festoon." Darker now. My face resembles trichinosis. Let the conundrums quiver! I second these minutes. Can anyone find the light switch?

Barbed wire, why so zealous? Why is the picnic basket charred? I hope a "bowl cut" will suffice. Soon your refrigerator full of lint will take flight, and that's when I'll bare real wounds, but in the meantime the Yes Man keeps shuffling these pages.

Did I tell you that Father has taken on the role of planetarium director? At first, the news was rather shocking, but then we realized how well he met the qualifications. As we know, planetarium directors are prone to incipient baldness. They have no appetite for rising action. H.O. trains circle deceptively deep puddles in their childhoods, and their lives appear tremulous—mostly because their spleens consist of terrycloth and chunks of feldspar—and their gaze has been described as "nouveau septic." From a distance, planetarium directors may be mistaken for peccadillos (the red-winged variety), which possibly accounts for their irresolute character and tendency to shrug inappropriately under stress. Little is known about their sexual mores or what they consider to be innuendo, and for that reason it is unwise to ask their opinions on anything.

Darker now. Were it not for poesy, our cheese would surely languish. Last night, the moon drank all my Milk of Magnesia. I dreamt of key fobs chirping like catbirds on a power line. Today the ditch is choking on violets, and my heart is dry tinder. Have we entered the infinitival mode? It's only fair to inform you that there's a waiting room behind my eyes, where my true soul sits cross-legged in flickering light (fluorescent, of course), eating mallow cups and undressing you ontologically until there's nothing left but a blue flame. Like Death, I chew with my mouth open, watching while an old woman paints marionettes in your image. The only question is "Is she in our heads, or are we in hers?"

Now a single black milkweed parachutes toward your open hand.

"Not darkness," says the worm. "You can *see* darkness."

7

Father is distributing allegories to the needy.

Father anoints with mercurochrome the balding pates of burgermeisters.

Father explains gyroscopes to children, speaking in measured cadences and pointing to the sky.

He says "Translucency." "Meek." "Atonement."

He says "Pestilence." "Beseech." "Mire."

Father collects the tears of grieving widows for his soup and solves quadratic equations on everybody's napkin.

Father points out a passing cloud to a stone.

Alone in the attic, Father tinkers with his silhouette; he glues tiny clock parts to an illuminated manuscript, humming softly as he works.

Whenever he is angry, Father wears a veil made of smoke.

Whenever he falls in love, Father sires an invisible son, whom he names "Timothy Paul."

Father is convinced that he knows moonlight "for what it is."

He says, "Cinder." "Invisible." "Bequeath."

He says, "Wound." "Raiment." "Slake."

Father believes it possible, given an infinity of time, to calculate pi's final integer but never to "know the mind of man."

Father dreams that he is a prophet with larvikite eyes and a beard of Saint Elmo's fire; he calls for public weeping to forestall the coming pestilence.

Father has taken to projecting imaginary galaxies on the planetarium's domed ceiling. "There is no 'outside' from which to observe the expanding universe," he announces, "nor can we explain why the rate of expansion seems to be increasing rather than slowing—which is why we posit phenomena such as 'dark matter' and 'dark energy.'"

Father worries that he's substituting feelings for belief. He wears a special "demythologizing" monocle, so that he won't confuse the lint in his pocket with stars.

Father carries a special key, which he uses to unlock the basement door.

He stands on the top stair, silhouetted in a rectangle of light. "Timothy Paul, come out of the root cellar," he shouts.

"Timothy Paul, this is your father."

"Timothy Paul, don't try to hide—I know you're down there."

8

Skating past your house at midnight, dog-whistle in hand, I ponder your unconcealment. Already a truculent rain is gathering itself inside a cloud;

soon it will ply lovers with its silver needles and cold exclamation points, making a sound like plangent harpsichords. I wipe away what spores I can and squint into the underbrush. Does the hooded falcon perched on my arm belong to you? Its talons seem to be drawing blood, though I doubt it's intentional. What's the name of that glove a falconer wears on his arm? A gauntlet? I should have one of those!

Was it Wittgenstein who said, "One observes in order to see what one would not see if one did not observe"? That reminds me: I think the milk's gone bad. Shall we blame the gibbous moon, the half-finished soup, your penchant for calculative thought? Whose turn is it to walk the dog? Am I ready for another "near-life" experience? Why am I bleeding myrrh? These gondolier costumes were your idea, don't forget! Watching you read Hegel's *Asthetik* while lying naked on high thread count sheets makes me wonder if it is possible to exist outside of description and narration. Why don't we pretend these constellations belong to us, the way words do when we think we've tamed them? After all, "anise" is just another name for fennel—or so you'd have me believe.

How shall we tally these unremembered dreams?

Are the final credits rolling so soon?

Mune, mune, mune, mune, mune! Jaundiced, bleary-eyed, drunk on fog! Does a blank stare count as the Other's gaze? You should know—you have the blankest stare of all—you half-eaten wafer, you old man's mirror, you broken compass—plagiarist of unfinished poems! Each night, you perform another cranioplasty. You peer into my skull and laugh as these dreams put my words through the spin cycle. You subject my dithyrambs to your gravitational force. You fill my head with silver commas. And now I wonder—why do you steep the faux roses in your amniotic light? Is that the shadow of your inconstancy I see in my lover's eyes?

"Good questions," says the Yes Man. He sets down a briefcase containing seventeen vials of rhino horn powder. "And I have a few questions of my own. For instance, 'Does God wait for us behind each closed door? Or is God the closed door itself?'"

"Irrelevant!" shouts Father. "What we want to know is, 'Where did this dark matter come from? Did someone forget to turn off the blender?' Well, moon, what do you say to that? I'll just chew on these faulty syllogisms and await your reply."

"Ignore them, moon," cries Mother. "You and I both know the real question seems to be 'Does this gravy need more salt?'"

We turn our expectant gazes skyward, as our kind has done for millennia. But the orphaned, heretical, dissolute moon shines down on all of us, or perhaps in spite of us—yes, even you, patient reader—and says nothing.

The Arena

#

I enter what some call "the arena."
Would you say that the radio is "tuned between stations"?
I dance in thin air above the sinkhole—which is to say I "acknowledge
    despair, and this alone makes gaiety possible."
Do you remember the time we read that a lover's body may be likened
    to "a palimpsest of texts"—some written *by* the body and others
    inscribed *upon* it? The trick, we learned, is telling which is which.
Consider yourself forewarned: this is not a love poem.
All of the "lyrical I's" have left for Des Moines.
The reader seeking eros, or even agape, may experience a dopamine shortage.
With that established, dearest, would you say I aspire to "radio silence"
    or "radio static"?
Did you know that "arena" means "sand-strewn"?
Don't read too much into the fact that night has fallen.
As I watch, the moon slips another ransom note under my pillow, but this
    is not that kind of poem, either.

#

The fields marked * are required.
This poem uses cookies. This poem would like to send notifications.
This poem would like to generate rhetorical antitheses and "culturally
    ordained binaries" set in opposition like "armed gladiators."
This poem would like to fail in its ontological striving.
This poem would like to leave late industrial capitalism unchanged.
What this poem assumes, you shall assume—though this poem respects
    the temporary accretion of perceptions that comprise your
    so-called "self," and offers a range of privacy options.
This poem would like you to remember sun dogs over Pensacola.
This poem would like you to remember what happened that night
    beneath the apple blossoms.
This poem would like to affect an Ovidian transformation of an imaginary
    lover into "trees, springs, rocks, flowers, rivers, or birds"—
but only to make a point about figurative language, since this poem
    is not a love poem.
Why must this poem keep reminding you of that?

#

I was too busy positioning the electrodes to note the color of his eyes.
I was too busy positioning the electrodes to gauge the thickness of her lips.
I was too busy positioning the electrodes to dial in the station that speaks
    for you—or vice versa.
"The purpose of the sand is to absorb blood," she crooned, proffering
    a sprig of dill to the assembled spectators.
I shall remain respectful of your jouissance throughout the surgical procedure.
Meanwhile, high above Des Moines, the moon turns to pumice
    everything it touches—
and so teaches us a valuable lesson about desire and loss.
Is it fair to say that, from our vantage point, this sinkhole resembles
    an archeological site?
Can you hear all the "writerly texts" murmuring from below?
Perhaps that moon and this sinkhole share certain traits which
    only a "former lover" is qualified to observe.
I was too busy positioning the electrodes to consider that possibility.

#

The reader is reminded that "some slippage is inevitable."
Don't read too much into the falling pocket watches.
I woke early, only to discover that someone had been tampering
    with my re-entry burns.
That was the year I lost my peripheral vision in the war.
Say, is this the station where all the voices are pre-recorded?
Is this the station where the music has blind spots?
Is this the station "structured like a language"?
Is this the station where I drive a blue car through your dreams?
"Get out of here with those shopworn tentacles," he cried, clutching
    a sprig of creeping bellflower.
The arena is no place for a lover's lament.
Ask anyone in Des Moines.

#

One narrator arrives, clean-shaven, carrying a black valise
    that contains a metalanguage.
He wants to argue that *every* play is "a play within a play."
Nevertheless, we remain trapped within the synecdoche of dreams.
Meanwhile, in Des Moines, where the diaphanous tastes of phosphor,
    an object-relations theorist's moon rises above the radio station.
Meanwhile, elsewhere in Des Moines, one former lover bleeds

morning glories.
We once read that the body is not a social construct, but all these
 words are—and the "selves" that we conjure by thinking
 with words are constructs, as well.
Welcome to the death of literature. Sorry, I meant "dearth."
Today I will calculate the ratio of barometric pressure to epistemological
 uncertainty—a relationship between physical and mental quanta
 in which old lovers play no part.
"I apologize for keeping you waiting, but the anesthesiologist is stuck
 in traffic," the surgeon muttered, waving a sprig of corn-cockle.
From Pensacola to Des Moines is 1,029 miles.
The sinkhole is becoming indistinguishable from the arena.

 #

Between the mute fire of nerves and the coil of memory: words
 and their endless deferment.
We are embodiments of words—words made flesh. Didn't we read
 that somewhere?
Jesus wept Velcro tears.
The poem refined its algorithm.
Allegorists are standing by to take your call.
Meanwhile in Des Moines, someone got the bright idea of opening
 a candelabra shop in the new strip mall—the one next to the landfill.
I'm ashamed to admit that my colleagues feel sorry for me,
 owing to this glandular condition, but it came in handy when
 I tried to strip-mine your affection. Who knew the run-off
 would be so toxic?
Last night I dreamt that it was night, and I was dreaming.
I woke to find myself surrounded by laughing narrators, riding
 in bumper cars, and eating cotton candy.
When they saw I was awake, they ripped off their monks' cowls
 and waved them overhead, shouting, "Hey, Bucky,
 haven't you heard? The unexamined life isn't worth living."
Then they laughed some more.

 #

The radio hisses.
Is this the station with random shocks?
"White noise consists of serially uncorrelated random variables," she cried,
 brandishing a sprig of lousewort.
This poem would like you to create an account.
This sinkhole would like you to stop dancing.
This moon would like you to acknowledge its tidal force on your dreams.
This narrator, bedecked in a robe of "purple furred velvet, welled with tinsel,"

would like to establish a reign of misrule throughout the text.
He says, "Did you know that Des Moines has the highest number
 of vacuum cleaner salesmen per capita?"
"Is that because of the lyrical I's?" I ask.
The narrator smiles and points a crooked finger at something
 neither of us can see.

#

"Excuse me, is this the way to the 'talking cure'?"
I was too busy positioning the electrodes to cordon off the aesthetic
 from the ethical.
When did your memento mori stop allegorizing?
When did your significant other stop signifying?
Meanwhile, high above Des Moines, the moon's image transformed
 itself into a referent.
That was the year I lost my aspect blindness in the war.
One narrator leans toward the mic and, in a voice mostly uvula, says,
 "Be our fifth caller and win a brand new lover of your dreams!
 That's caller number five."
I feel some counter-transference coming on.
I feel my re-entry burns starting to glow.
I feel like touching that dial. I feel like changing stations.
I feel like taking this vacuum cleaner attachment and bludgeoning
 caller number five.

#

Don't read too much into the falling apple blossoms.
Don't read too much into the floating candelabras.
Don't read too much into the dyspeptic figures.
Don't read too much into the overflowing jouissance.
Here above the sinkhole, one can read from top to bottom as well as
 left to right. But what, exactly, does such a reading entail?
Furthermore, what constitutes the "bottom"?
"Perhaps these words form a paratext, floating like a sun dog beside
 a 'main text' that is not yet visible," she said, unfurling
 a sprig of clasping henbit.
I was too busy positioning the electrodes on caller number five
 to decode her remark.
"...which is precisely why you need a metalanguage," said the narrator,
 popping the latches of his black valise. He opened the lid
 and waved his hand in the air with a flourish. "Voilà."
I peered inside. "But these are just more ransom notes," I protested.
The reader is reminded that "some slippage is inevitable."

What remains once the "effects of marketing" are removed?
Was it Rimbaud who said, "All moons are painful"?
This poem would like you to savor its bouquet of resemblances.
As we watch, the Lyrical I's, wearing robes of ambient light, gather
        outside the antechamber, singing the old hymn,
            "Time Is Syntax, Unfolding Inside Us."
Meanwhile in Des Moines, I have a recurring dream about parthenogenesis.
        All I remember is that you're not in it.
That was the year I lost these anachronisms in the war.
Say, is this the station with encroaching margins?
Do her virescent eyes' anonymous horizons beckon you, like a shadfly
        to a streetlamp?
Look! Do you see that narrator dragging Allegory behind him
        on silver chains? He would like to impart a few words
which you will probably perceive as echoes, and which will leave
        an aftertaste of forgotten wine in your throat.
Don't be surprised if it leaves you thirstier than before.

Effulgence at Three O'Clock

"The chief difficulty Alice found at first was in managing her flamingo." —Lewis Carroll

    1

Two lovers en-
twined by
the quarry's edge:
(read "foaming sighs")
(read "lyrical glaze")
—the curiously inwrought
figurations
"when the illegible becomes pellucid"
as or as if
(O apostrophe—to whom I know not—)
this decorative abyss
in love with
easeful
decolletage
sans
"the disenchantments of the world"
(read "tinfoil moons")
(read "pensive roses")
(read "dirty sparrows")
(read "cardboard Venus")
or ask, "Is that Chinese lantern
imaginary?
Is this
silhouette
crouching in what you call
'the background'
merely an astigmatic shadow?"
i.e.,
"do irredeemable diadems
drop
unbidden?"
as or as if
the poem's potential auditors—
a necessary subterfuge—

actually ex/ist
"so long lives this"
(read "his lambent heart")
(read "the dream-lit arbor")
(read "her eyes at neap tide")
(read "flamingo of your—")
"curious dints"
—words channeling desire—
"upon a table"
as or as if
"the hedgehog had unrolled itself"
in lyre-prismed
"boxes of cerebration"
Into which
the flamingo slips
("such a puzzled expression")
almost unseen
its pink feather
so that
"she could not help
bursting out laughing"
and
"it was a very difficult game indeed."

   2

Say a "real" quarry
is made allegorical
by the lovers' proximity
(or vice versa?)
as or as if
the gaping pit
false azure
a symphony of nerves
whose third movement—"a
boisterous scherzo"—
plays out
in georgic tableaus
("You are old," said the
shepherd youth)
repeatedly
which is to say
"One of the lovers could be you!"
If you
suspend
time or

"Now I'll manage better"
as or as if
run simulacra
(read "sad balconies"
(read "nightingales on strings"
(read "Death's hand-puppets"
(read "memory-foam heart"
the lyric already de-
centered
preceding
commodifying
inventing
"love"
"the silken dénouement"
of "'homestyle' aphrodisiacs"
woven
O Ever-Absent
thinking Itself
as or as if
quarried
querying
uni-
verse
sans
sans
as or as if
allegories
wake us and we en-
twine
where ne'er the twain
shall meet

    3

(read "his battery-operated bloodstone"
(read "her periwinkle herring"
(read "his synecdochic dowsing"
(read "her photosynthetic inculcation"
(read "his splenetic peripheries"
(read "her dulcet phlebotomies"
(read "his warrantless panegyrics"
(read "her saturnine incubators"
as or as if
borders sealed
devil's playground of
verbal hedges, shibboleths, all the

"latest formulations"
run simulacra
"You are old"
sans
flocks
you are
"written to nobody
which isn't usual"
said the King
or would you rather
think in greeting card slogans
run on verbal donut-tires
dine on TV dinners
limit reflection to "selfies"
as or as if
"Eat your Jell-O, Reginald"
simply
tabulate
pleasures & pains
all your so-called
life
and
"If you cannot afford a poet,
one will be appointed to you"
so
just a reminder
you are scheduled
for effulgence
at three o'clock
please
have your
flamingos ready.

Dopic

Dopic (also "doplic"): a Pennsylvania Dutch term, derived from the German "doppich," meaning "clumsy or awkward," used primarily in Central and Southeastern Pennsylvania.

"I work from awkwardness. By that I mean I don't arrange things. If I stand in front of something, instead of arranging it, I arrange myself." —Diane Arbus

Dopic conjures lesser trombones. He bites too hard on marmalade.

Dopic trips because the world is clumsy. He watches the sky for falling pianos and searches his words for sinkholes.

Dopic cannot see from one end of memory to the other. Does this explain why he's dopic? He knows that every thought is a burnt bridge, already belated, yet he suspects that knowing this changes nothing.

"Life is a blade," says Dopic, "and hunger's the whetstone."

On good days, Dopic is a philanthropist, distributing shadows to the snow-blind. Given the chance, he will weave a school administrator's syllogisms into dreamcatchers. On other days, Dopic forgets what it is he should have done—and these days are becoming more frequent.

Dopic observes the girl with the origami heart waiting in the rain, but he can't recall her name.

Dopic believes that the visual field extends to peripheries we do not "look at" but rather "sense" with a vague sort of attention—and this accounts for his vacant stare. As for the world, Dopic would like to "fit in," though what he's fitting into isn't exactly clear. Until he can figure it out, he spends his time studying x-rays of the moon and arguing prognoses with moths.

Dopic is growing old. Sometimes he worries that his desire has become too Pythagorean. Is this why he prefers to stand on parapets—the better to see the abstractions overtaking him? Is this why he often wonders whether two rights make a wrong, whether the soul is a prime number, or whether it's possible to explain what a clock is to the desert?

One thing is certain: Dopic is never there when money changes hands.

"Dopic! Why must you be so dopic?" says Mother. Kitchy koo. Kitchy kitchy koo.

"Dopic, you must remember that 'Thought's detours become the body's road,'" says Father. "Don't you think it's time to get back on the path and let the Good Book be your guide?"

Dopic wonders if his stigmata should come with laugh tracks. As he waits for darkness to eat the crumbs he leaves behind, Dopic comes to understand that a man can never find refuge in his own shadow—not even at night, not even with his glow-in-the-dark Jesus on the nightstand.

Dopic tries to comprehend the nature of Being, but he can't get past all those gerunds.

Dopic hates closure. He has come to realize that both the pearl and the poem are born of irritants. (Is that why he spends his days trying to rehearse non-sequiturs?)

"Writing a poem is like lugging a bell up a hill," says Dopic.

The girl with the origami heart says nothing. What else did he expect?

Sometimes at night Dopic listens to the ocean, which sounds like a radio tuned between stations. "How can death be said to ease life's pain when there is no "self" left to perceive that the pain is gone?" he wonders, but without his monocle, Dopic finds it hard to speculate further. Isn't that always the case?

Thinking of his own death, Dopic tries to outstare the open door, the clock, the mirror. He tries to count the serpent tongues whispering in his brain. He makes a motion to adjourn, but nobody seconds.

Sometimes Dopic recounts the many things he has seen, or thinks he's seen: schoolboys huffing nacre in blind alleys, morticians tying blood knots, sun dogs over Pensacola, an angel peeling its own skin out of despair for love. He can still recall childhood, with its black web of cricket sound above the turnip fields and the conflagration of roses outside his bedroom window. He can still remember the terraced light of an August morning and the hormonal Tristan chords of adolescence playing through his body, though now they seem more like phantom pain.

More recently, Dopic has grown tired of tallying afterglows. "It's like spoon-feeding pieces of myself to jackals," he says to no one there. (Dopic often speaks to no one there; he's become a master soliloquist-- the Hamlet no one overhears.)

Still, Dopic tries not to talk with his mouth full. He closes his eyes and feels the moon spreading its pathogens through his heart and lungs, his liver and his spleen, his kidneys, his teeth, his bowels. It's how he knows he's still here.

These days, Dopic can no longer find sheep's clothing that fit. He still refuses to swear a loyalty oath; instead, he wants to burn every doily in sight.

Perhaps this accounts for the fact that he's come to prefer the jeremiad to the panegyric, or that he cannot trust a poem that doesn't have zippers.

Dopic believes that the moon is the sun's catachresis—and he should know! But don't ask him to explain, especially now, as he is sprawled naked on a sun dial, humming a tune from 1974, and waiting for the imaginary guests to arrive. At such times, it is best not to disturb him. And of course no one would, for they know that if they do, Dopic might come hurtling toward them through a wormhole made of words.

Oof!

1

Together we watched the tipple boy traipse across the shag, clutching fistfuls of thrip-infested henbit in his pale fingers—but because there was no suede to be found, Mother developed a lisp. Consequently, her zigzag appeared roseate, and her smile brightened the room like a New Mexico lighthouse. Oof! Is it any wonder that I reached puberty in a skating rink, encircled by illuminati wearing see-through eyepatches, or that I couldn't find my prosthetic aura? Someone had shrink-wrapped my succor and sucked down Aunt Hecuba's "special broth," which is known to induce verisimilitude—the kind that neuters memory and leaves us gasping in our own wakes. You remember Aunt Hecuba, don't you? She's the one who veiled herself in chintz.

2

Seen from above, these spirals look like circles. Has anyone ever told you that, and if so, what color was their hair? Who hasn't felt the night's dribs and drabs, or watched in dismay as his butterscotch develops fever blisters? Can no one tell me why speleologists disdain slumber parties? "The spirit soars the more it weighs and sinks into itself," says Vallejo. Oof! Is that the sort of lyricism you seek? Sometimes I wake with a chameleon's tail clenched between my teeth, and your smile is like moonlight reflected in a scimitar. I guess that's why thinking of you is like trying to parse liquid mercury. I guess that's why you remain mum on the subject of flywheels. But the night's calipers will take our measure, and soon another dream will reach out with transparent tentacles, leaving us "beset by feelings," awash in shimmering treacle. But the opalescence will not last—even though we imbue our discourse with what might charitably be called "afterglows." And once it fades, there's nothing left but to loiter on horizons, watching our failings puddle as these thrips multiply exponentially. Oof! Oof! How is it that your eyes caused my heart to suffer rope burn fifty years ago, and yet this pain outlives us, the way music outlives its instruments?

3

Do you see how my broken stick stirs the well water, releasing gray-crested birds with black beaks into a starving sky?

They say a man who breaks forms is often broken by them.

I say, "Stab chrysanthemums where it counts!" For one never knows when the next generation of demi-gods may appear, and the face of reality transforms itself. Ah, the new reality, with its chitinous thorax and quantum eyes! The new reality, with its lard-covered zeal! The new reality, with its Spartan ammonias and imaginary vowels, its humming crystals and gift shop incense, its silvery perpendiculars and valet parking, its seraph mazes, its bashful curls, its uncrossed legs and periodic charts and Persian whispers—will it overturn the old Laws of Attraction, or will it condense them into a clock of words? Will it unleash an army of palindromes across the feathered plain? Or will the moon, in a fit of pique, rain homonyms upon the unsuspecting hordes?

O demi-gods, come to us with your Pythagorean hosannas. Enucleate our eidos. Comb gravity into furrows, that our love may run straight and deep and our poems radiate what the blurb writers call "revelatory beauty," "exceptional grace," "valiant wit," "lyrical intensity," "unalloyed pleasure," "thunderous emotional resonance," "an ideal permanence," and "sheer good nature." Reduce us to glowing nubs. Knock, breathe, shine, and seek to mend. Tear down the gibbets and fumigate every aftermath, so that unrequited lovers may cease their tiresome processionals, bearing plastic lilies and shower attachments past the altar of Mouth-Breathing Desire as part of some emotional Tenebrae ceremony. Cut to the gizzard those who don time's vestments and pass them off as wizard cloaks. Grant us our suede. Parse our suffering. And tell the tipple boy to wipe his shoes.

4

It was time to suture our embouchures together.

Then it was past time.

And then your memory turned to stone.

Thus, in love's wake, I found myself sleep-walking through the aviary, chanting doxologies and painting imaginary holes in the ceiling, and it was at this time I encountered a pale stranger who could have been your dead brother. He stared at my shoes as if he'd fallen in love with them. "A trail of salt leads to a trail of cinders, which leads to a trail of ashes, which leads, in turn, to self-knowledge," he said, bending down to touch my laces. "Of course, the self-knowledge is of a kind that no one can use—hence, its claim to truth."

"Keep your vanishing points to yourself," I screamed.

Only then did I realize that the Greek chorus which had been accompanying me had mysteriously departed, wrenching my actions free of social context. Oof!

My sheep's clothing no longer fit.
I gazed up at the gloating moon.

Inside my mouth, a new tongue was already starting to burn.

    5

The imaginary guests arrive at four.

Then will come a parting of veils, and mirrors will turn transparent.

My solar plexus will become a tuning fork, and this silver whistle, which you once wore on a chain around your neck during calisthenics, will summon a new generation of poets, misshapen by neglect, their grudges bound in copper wire. Then we'll all shrug in unison, and the search for suede and uninfected henbit will resume as if nothing had happened—which seems a reasonable hypothesis.

Still, so many questions remain, growing ever more strident: why does God allow my palette to go uncleansed? Why is your tremendous outpouring espaliered? Why are we the only ones without a credo?

Look! Do you see how that little cloud blocks the moon? Well, I say, "It's about time!" After all, haven't we had enough of the scaly moon with its laudanum beams, the pock-faced moon upon which so many misguided subjectivities are projected (to no useful end), the carpet-cleaning, obfuscating moon with its silent percolations and penchant for turning fresh croissants a wan shade of blue? Oof! Damn straight we've had enough! Light of false prophets, distorter of memory, be gone!
Much obliged, little cloud!

    6

Why is it when I think of you, the subjunctive always slithers in? Is it because my despair is more French than yours? To be fair, your Teutonic despondencies never fail to send salacious shivers through the ranks of the poetasters, but this begs the question: what is the nature of poetic discourse? Is it a cause or an effect? And how shall we distinguish perception from interpretation? That I create or summon these images to perpetuate you, the phantasm that animates them, is perhaps the salient point—though like all points, it is dimensionless. Oof! I guess I'll go on planting larkspur in your footprints. I guess I'll think about your eyes as I chew on another votive candle. It's like the Lutherans say: "Memory-brine makes for salty soup; hence, one should never wear suede on the beach." But enough fashion tips. The guests will soon be here, and Mother is cooking up something liminal. Can't you smell the ontology wafting through the vestibule, causing small hairs to rise? And in her "attic kitchen," Aunt Hecuba is coaxing syncopation from a pair of oversized maracas while humming "Begin the Beguine" softly to herself. Like the rest of us, she is waiting for something to boil.

 7

Treefrogs are less succinct in their salted vespers than I in this, my plainsong, O translucent amour! Come out to this screened-in patio, adjacent to my domicile; together we can dine on Pringles and American cheese. Quell your saturnine harangues and allow me to bloviate in my defense, for it is nearly dark, and the cicadas are lowing. April's crinoline has given way to July's gabardine, and even now Cupid is gargling in the bulrushes. O would that I could touch you, my impeccant toad lily. I mean empirically. For truly the glaze is on the onion, and night draws nigh, with its Jack-in-the-box music and pointed questions: Will your kisses taste the way these locusts sound? Will this itching prove chthonic? Will these fireflies in my brainstem be enough to light our way? Oof! Take me now, before Time gavels in the next dramatic irony! Leave me beset with squints, hog-tied to your memory. Berate me with your silent bells.

 8

"As long as man keeps hearing words/ he's sure that there's a meaning somewhere." Mephistopheles (from Goethe's *Faust*).

It wasn't my turn to defamiliarize the roses.

Your tongue grafts didn't take.

Did she come undone at the twitch of a diphthong? Did he arrive at his idea of beauty using "the subtractive method"?

People who always ask, "What does it mean?" seldom know what they mean by "mean."

Even now, their small pulleys perform obstetric maneuvers silently, without expression, but the tipple boy, asleep on a bed of straw, lowers silver plumb lines into trillium dreams.

 9

Imagine a harpsichord thrown down a stairwell. Imagine your elbows and knees exchanging places. Imagine an explosion in the xylophone factory or jet-skiing on the Lethe. Imagine turning the word "thwart" over and over in your mouth until it assumes a gelatinous quality.

"Arriving from always, you'll go away everywhere," says Rimbaud.

What time does the theme park open?

What constitutes verisimilitude, and is it more dependent on the laws of genre than it is on reality (the "referent") itself?

A gravedigger rearranged the lexicon while my back was turned. A few meanings, still damp with significance, slipped into the cracks. All the great ideas stood in ruins like rows of broken teeth, as a pack of developmental psychologists picked through the rubble, making high-pitched bird-like noises. Hoping to be of assistance, I took up crocheting Rorschach yarn-blots, but everybody clicked their tongues and accused me of "object hunger."

Now, due to the suede shortage, I am unable to fully submit myself to language. Due to the suede shortage, I can no longer remember the way to Porlock. Due to the suede shortage, your secondhand lotus will have to suffice. Shall I scramble the codes altogether? Oof! Oof! Oof! Oof! Oof! What gilds these recollections, these endless gerunds of lack? Is it poetry? Is this a memory because you are in it? Now spring sounds its muddy trumpet, the henbit yawns into blossom, and an old man's thoughts turn to "personal subjective transformation." Cheese Nips, anyone? Do you prefer thrips or Furies? There are myths that make our footnotes bristle—yet most of our memories are "personal," tied to the pH factors of individual moments. Only a few seem linked to a narrative that defines us. Therefore, the "semiotically dispersed subject" in me is compelled to ask, "Is it not in memory that the world's inscriptions become legible?"

"Hold that thought," says the gravedigger. "My shift is over, so let's pick this up next time."

Next time? I must say, I admire his optimism! *Next time*—when the flywheels turn for us alone, when we dwell in an effulgence of suede and our pain no longer outlives us. *Next time,* with its zither music and manganese promises. *Next time,* with its brain tinsel and shimmering calyx. Whether "next time" awaits us on oblivion's far shore, I cannot say. So until we meet again, adieu, adieu, my little pistachio, my frantic bouillabaisse! Let me say in parting that you remind me of my secret mother and father, the quiet ones who built clocks using tiny magnets and the bones of mice.

Famous Last Words

First Series

#1 (12/19-20/2021)

Remember their names—these pink situationists "crazy for you"
aching because the pale evenings adumbrate your dumb anguish   sunder
    the twilight
and map voices untranslatable   I hear them talking here in untied night
I see the moon's membrane   a hapless angel aching   yet I "do not
    understand"
beyond summer's mere breeze   the Narcissus pool   the cloaked briars
the mad unknown heart   and the lamp "no brain can contain"
These pages burn intense red   O Mnemosyne   as if unuttered
nothing to repeat but these rushing sounds announced by small mouths
plangent annotations dribbled into dust   echoes from sleep that heave
    aside the hour
On the white shore behind the mirror a signature awaits   Am I coming
    home nameless?
The smallest rain is dreamed into substance   the blank stone goes
    unremembered
shivering absence mixes darkly with Philosophy's void   dust, sun, time
reflected in the still point beyond ultimate things   what remains disappears
The holy is what is eclipsed   behind the door

#2 (12/21-22/2021)

You step willingly through illusions of ash   mad sleeping alphabets   bone-texts
The script's inky reaches   a paradigm of summer written backwards
remembering who I am   Why announce it whose purpose is nothing but
    alphabet noise?
A name's weight   the clime to which the hallowed brain clings   asleep
    dancing its patterns
I am wandering forever where the stones promise not a sentence   my gyre
    whitened
this small "now" caught in the undertow   moving in the opposite direction
My sky comes undone in a hitch-hiker's dream   confused by time   My
    flesh like tiny moons
scattered by sudden surrealism   suffers pronoun drowsiness in a phonebooth
Am I between answers?   A corpse out of range of postmodernism?
Between blanche and blank   the dreary text proceeds unfinished
What are the stars a poet demands?   This broken glass pointillism   itself

       a dereliction
groping nevertheless toward a lightless Flame   inchoate   cannot name it
cannot name this wound that was us   its rage tossed upon the so-called Self
its echoes plunging into an ancient book   of limitless equivocation

#3 (12/22/2021)

You sought the Muses on the puzzled page   cold and causeless
asleep   dreaming of dead book-spines and insubstantial summer light
        dissolved in
the dark cradle of memory   Your eye painted the imaginable dust   mist
        and shadow
Your brain   waterswept as Ophelia   garlanded with desire's dead wreaths
lingered among the ghosts and running figures of a text   before sinking
        into ink
on a page unnumbered   And these whispered imitations singing you to
        unexamined places
(as if life were a labyrinth of magazines thumbed-through   and not ineffable
        and oblique
its distances fluid and indistinct)   become self-indulgent   reminding you
to remember your heart   that unintelligible sleeping Judge   with his mouth
        worn off
always displaying a still-life of the "other" whose name entwined with yours
followed by an innuendo   There is no rationale for Night's song
with its itchy syntax and Latin apocalypses   its little unseen crimson nebulae
its prism of silence   its fluid antimonies   its slow limbo and array of mirrors
on an ancient black hill   flickering in the distance before you   never to be
        written

#4 (12/22-23/2021)

Adolescent lust   with its false eyelashes   and masturbation-into-smoke
its shattered crystal   fireflies burning and pronouns indistinct
—synapse-perplexing and yet   all beautiful   until its lap-dancing light
        disappears
and her altar is called into question   Then your mad eyes turn to hell   You think
        about it
riding lips, hand, sky   arrhythmia of mental pubis in perpetuum   on spent
        graying celluloid
like a prayer fretted through a chasm   shadow play and nothing in an instant
your moth-mind blank on arrival   But when love's "sign" changes   there is
        no other recourse
I dress you up in skin   inky stranger   I mean clothes   I mean words
        words words

singing your existence into assumed shapes   your opaque Venus dress
beautiful celestial vehicle   knowing the essential soup   water, dust, stars
mouth-eating gods   dark matter   and dreams darker still   darker than
        mirrors inside out
These vowel rivulets through breath borne to the sea   these distances the
        poem recalled
This body unremembered   Let the gods beware our names   these ashes
        in the mouth
Pure knowledge illumines what it annihilates   "being" and "heaven" beyond
        our ken

#5 (12/23/2021)

Marvelous and empty   the torn book   talking vertigo   with its wasteland
        of poetry schemes
its possibilities of grass   (the "lawn within")   speaks to absent clouds the way
oneiric angels outside the pharmacy murmur to designated drivers in
        sentences null and void
How measure the clock, the albatross, the irregular verbs?   A page is
        always missing
Each persona is merely a fulcrum while habit does the speaking   and the past
is what you say "death" with   and therefore I pretend you are still here
with your candy hearts and straws   new skin dissolving in a wake of
        yellow whorls
feigning tenderness on stage but never waking behind the mask   every word
        a vacuum
You are the hole I cannot undo   In these dead passages the white stain
        is there
Our pronouns reverse   I see the other me in a green haze plying paramours
        in tired reruns
Overwhelming nostalgia appears as a glycerin cloud of looming gnats
In my untoward reflection the wax seal of memory recalls love rituals gone
        fatally wrong
The Hour of Null halves itself   In the lit Palace of Nothing there are only
        voices

#6 (12/23-25/2021)

In the labyrinth we witnessed pronoun lightning through the alphabetical array
the sliding words resounding and forgotten   memory's husks   troubadour skulls
My sleep was offered up nightly to the tiny god of stairways   A stranger
        with burnt fingertips

dedicated his life to Eros   We witnessed Heraclitus catching fire   and heard
 ghost echoes
dreaming through closed dictionaries   Such particulars give birth to the moon
which adorns the darkened areas   shedding lost clues and movie-screen
 reveries
(no memory afterwards   just vagabond time and the self alone no camera
 captures
making oblations to invisible bodies and to the tiny god of stairways   which is me
a solar flare partaking of a dream)   And the soul's syncope   marginless
 and immaterial
like an unaccented syllable or unfinished bridge   stretches toward its false
 eternity
beyond frameworks of reference and the dusty reaches of conjecture
And the red ghosts drink names   Sirens in the fog promise salvation
The eye in the mirror mask sees the text's body written backwards
Mapping the way to the abandoned chapel where her floating name creases
 heaven

Second Series

#7 1/13/2022

Upon hearing giants, give vent   O milky precipitate   ring the doorbell of one who lives here
I first exhaled pleasure in the shallows of a major oeuvre   another time, perhaps?
The meaning of dreams encumbering cornucopias   dancing in hotel rooms
Forever for now   the usual intervals and spectacularly boring egg   life a pinprick
The warning signs are important   everybody was expecting you   to be laid out
Reflected in the window of the city at the end of the fiscal year   as behooves us, surely
Bantamweight highwaymen off the scent at last   antithesis of distinction   this
Confused canal of references and self-imaginings   laughably wrong pop-ups
Swizzle sticks gazed at directly from the wings by an old actor drunk on love   so blue and
Understaffed   I recommend it highly   wintery scenes with their thickets of promise
Reception seemed viable as darkness came unknotted and saints went back to the basics
The lobby of history   annals and weathervanes   pointing backwards   some pretext
Or bewildering formulation   the birds, silent and analytical   wheedle on
Remnants of February about to chime   light pouring from the master's hand

#8 1/13/2022

The doghouse was dark   surrounded by the real   your fears seemed justified
Shrinking into the edge of the "other" garment   clouds in the yard   drizzle
On porch chairs   signs   (signs?)   (of America?)   thirty-year-old ashtray
Dandelions and filling stations   lips of my late employer   stones piled up
Deep ribbons fall from heaven like August's last geranium   resembling molded fire
Father in his little house of parchment   where ailments dwell   (I was leaving anyway)
Miserable town of tar and imbroglios   ravenous   overstuffed   (yet threadbare)
Veils pierced with sighs   not enough time before the monotonous embrace

    of death
So many things I would rather be doing   jumping off a cliff   seminars
    laundry
The attention bares its teeth   unbuttoned explanations spill like counterfeit
    jewels
Critical consent   words written down   snowing rubber bands like iridescent
    filaments
Supplicants on the shore of delirium lack capes or even undergarments
    the wind
Blew them apart   the pain of narrative (your punching ball) recedes   the
    fat lady hiccups
The conductor at the end of a long queue   with his obsolete radio   pro-
    claims bliss

#9 (1/13/2022)

Ancient man   religious animal beneath unsuitable heaven   writing things
    for me (you)
Death sound falling on white tiles   existence under the umbrella against
    afternoon light
Naming me just as the missing letter mounts the wound   the paper traps
    ill-lit scrolls
Terminal thoughts you pull out of the mirror (like a prayer's painted corners)
    dark blood
Of open books   on the polished floor   dark ice glittering on an already
    absent swan
As September breezes exalt the blank tulips of her eyes (i.e. "denote the
    presence")   or
The fountain   that broke when you entered it   the enormous word that
    can destroy us
Immortal music   the problem has not been solved   the love letters writing
    you (me)
Whitened   weeding out the heart's porphyry   so the phantom hungers
    may begin
Thus   what I say is in-between these lines   the sound of shadow   faded
    into light
(the old man managed to finish the sentence)   (the girl the old man ignored
    was set adrift)
(the paper trails changed the times we live in)   (the hole ran over us an
    hour earlier)
The loom   the factory   the jar   the violent birds   the ancient blue
    smoke   the tide
Oh heart ever-present   filling rapidly   and all your deeds sentenced in
    frozen ink

#10 (1/14/2022)

Our love balloons sometimes   I see your father's monocle has escaped his kindly eye
No reason to suppose he is playing a game   vigorously asserting the unsuitable figures
Dust, honey, elixir   another place grown smaller in an inconstant universe lost newsprint
And a telephone directory   "Prefer the new, old man!"   doubts come and hit you,
Which is why synonyms are used (indulge the thesaurus)   not enough time for an illustration
(or whatever truth is in season)   (apologias for embracing noumena and the mind's wet lakes)
(dumb oasis)   (surprise nap)   (you overstepped your haven—no way she spoke!)
(utterly crass sign)   unthinking fog from a wooden mouth   ritual abandonment
His life explained in engraved sobs   night hunger   the little chain of memory left
A page folded over   cold opal glare of naked couples beneath hollyhocks ruining your eyes
Terrifying obsolete flowers spring to mind (with a hiss)   landscapery changing to a strict green
I'm running out of mind-crystal   dry leaves coming at the end of sleep's revolving door
Return to the echoes that make us blue   loose-skinned anomalies   no permanent address
Fright-wigs of "meaning"   blocked access   a searchlight sweeping the reappearing bridge

#11 (1/15/2022)

The string quartet emergency brake vouchsafed our commitment   or lack thereof
It lay silent   weighted down with paperwork while the government went in
To build a thinktank   and the king's moustache turned fifty   (not your concern)
We were accustomed to stuttering there   porch-sitting our specialty   or so it is written
Better than brine or ice the terrifying sleep of love took her bearings   toxic cafeterias
A concrete image that symbolized her intentions   her uncertain chewing now public!
Screaming "Memory's a pickpocket!"   (the survivors will never know what we accomplished)

Therefore beneath the half-tones of a partial eclipse my appetites are good as new
A dragon passes over the sewers   the pensioners have gathered in the loggia
The ornamental wreckage having been replaced by another meaning   laminated mediocrity
Fluke, grave, needle   a flood of pagodas   backfiring flesh wounds   tragic stew on exhibit
(and its abominable antithesis)   the wheel much larger now   and reddening
Those woods being for many years part of some map   these jewels unbuttoned
These bankers rising   under such conditions no one took the architecture seriously

#12 (1/15/2022)

I see there is an intermission   in the American fashion   an expectation of disappointment
and I wanting the procession of lamps!   the lewd diversion!   martins falling from blue trees
in dark gardens!   "Lost words must have motion," says the accurate one musing on syntax
before dissolving in mists in the yard   was it merely a gesture   confused in summer light?
I remember the wrong dreams and the nasturtiums by the bulletin board and the temptress
With her press agent and specially built furnace   how they whispered opinions
While pissing on a rock   pledging not to return   hence my loathing for history
And the petal-blackened mainland with its tax-assessment area had grown wrinkled
Where sunlight fell   as I glimpsed you   chained to an aurora   the way we used to be
When each day seemed distinct as "other" words   far away   where true fragments light up
There is time enough for death's capacious billows   but for now all the factories are lit
The blind enemy who is to come sleeps in his cave   the useless mystery's mere condensation
Golden and pale   perfectly humdrum   will not express surprise at your absence
Yes the same one from which you began   cleansed of afterthought on the appointed day

#13 (1/17/2022—1/18/2022)

Sunlight fell into the night—that thief of colors—when you and I were young
The other way disappears   a welter of egoistic confusion already past
And you have come far indeed   the human mind with its dismal two-note
     theme
The narrow cement mixer noiselessly pouring its abundant sap   desires not
     yet pulsing
Not yet born   unwished-for   calling attention to the carnivorous but
     happy crowd
Inventing image-bubbles and phony explanations in a foreign language
     (mazy business)
Vanishing points in books and other contraptions of my own invention   effer-
     vescing liquid
Jets of fire   white tissue paper   the dubious surfaces   invisible writing
     in a darkened room
Half asleep   your dreams appear to become smaller and your line of sight
     dwindles
In hollow stones from my earliest childhood   the west wind of sexual
     imagery
"The real reality" of inner significance   distinctly visible   from this desert
     island nest
Our lives in its coils   the monotony of daily consciousness casting gray
     shadows
And the filthy slush of headlines lingers on in the wet part of our lives
     known as existence
The place where nothing happens   pushing to the very end your ecstasy
     and apprehension

#14 (1/19/2022)

Late this year, the climax of your casual quietude came loose   Too afraid
     to hire a workman
you shouldered the fragmentary masonry   kept body and soul underwater
     the pages
of your book above a sill   The way is clear to breathe in the night to come
     and day exhaled
In a landscape   the doubtful plain   the frightened river   those leaves
     presumed dead
The crater of evening with its little spurt of destiny leads to thoughts of
     a mind on the margin
or a crooked furrow   the promise of learning good reason to remain
     cowering
Thinking ahead   the presence of it "later on"   becomes another lesson
     on paper

Doorbells ring in the dark   expectation of annual rainfall is fulfilled   the way
          you used to do
The sky's unseen illustrations recall the way we used to live   wheeling
          aimlessly   self-evident
In our urgent masks   plotting itineraries with discernible motives like
          "memory for profit"
Man and wife cancel each other out as if charged by the thrill of the eidolon
With invisible markings   the smile of unforgettable questions   teeth and
          blood
The trajectory of things (particular of number) sprinkles the trees with
          verisimilitude
Everything is a landscape   until the idea itself is spattered by innumerable
          waves

#15 (1/20/2022)

The number which surrounds us is beautiful   the trajectories of indescribable
          fineness
Isolated instances perceived with a passive coherency might find your forehead
Yet we turn (hair awash) to the shore   the beaches   the warm day of
          nameless things
Under the umbrella of information that crumbles into life   (a book doesn't
          count)
The argument lifted out of the sea   where we left off only yesterday
          scratched
The plainer meaning of it (part of the next lesson) intentional in its aimlessness
The words boarded up   no design sticks   what remains is no parking space
No mountain (but a few stone markers)   the wind suspended   the actual
          closeness
Of a true source (divine in itself) long forgotten because all our lives we were
Watching our salary   bumming along yet continuing to exist   caught in
          that trap
That dream of enduring far into the blackness curling down   that unites us
          on its own terms
The record of summer totally subsumed   (would you check the time!)
          those feelings
You might think to be history may be allowed, at the end   they will seem
          like a joke
The final story will remain and memory strum its lyre at the edge of our days

#16 (1/20/2022)

Submerge personality in the exaggerated pumice of old sensations   most
          difficult

To recognize oneself becoming a medium   a floating one   in a self-induced
    trance
In the sun-lit mall   where your unhealthy repose (in which you are secure)
    goes unpunished
Tethered to a better sky beyond all dream of enduring   half my face
    thinking about you
Half my face happy with the result   the blind side first seeing the light
    now wishing to gaze
At your spun-out days in the September sun   all rusted and red   joy and woe
On their scented course along the empty routes of your final story   (including
    its stains)
The afternoon wind is making its rounds again   a discourse without end
    whose breath
Is so close   desperately sleeping   the rectangular shapes of quiet knowledge
(or whatever you wanted to call them)   down the drain   like nineteenth
    century romanticism
With its falsetto scenery and wise hymns   its alps and thresholds and rivers
    on both sides
Like water through a sieve   mesh of things of which it's written "There is
    no going back"
"There can be no further 'realistic noons'"   so you knew the folly and doom
    remained
Constructions to hold on to   the first danger sign like a stranger's forced
    handshake

Third Series

#17 (1/20/2022)

I see you   staring at the late afternoon's dazzle   the blue rain and black wheels
even I can't reach   no words to realize "truth"   just these blood-red wounds
(the only flames in a dark life)   inked upon the flesh   a demonstration
that our answers float out of sight   beyond saying   though both of us prayed to our gods
and loved the world we stayed to watch   the moon, the garden, our little loves lost
along the path   the old thirsts one wished enough and which   you'll agree   never were
the firmament's bright doors   shimmering   one step closer   (a creation all our own)
the yellow lines on new asphalt   the vacant houses and policy recommendations
the thieves and empty kingdoms   the dirty glass and the battlefield where no angels came
all this I have shown you   though you will always make it yours   burning as it is built
never once imagining all things were possible   which perhaps is why you grow silent
and a lasting guilt is born   like snow falling through any December   freezing the ground
and the wide bare sky   like words that cannot be unsaid   like the wakeful stars
like a small clock behind a shut door   just down the hallway of an endless dream

#18 (1/21/2022)

Father's punctual cigarettes still burn on the pavement where he let them fall.
The horizon in his eyes grows emptier as old age comes.
He does not realize that he is hidden   that the last word is spoken
but his nerves shimmer without rest like hummingbirds
and his fingers trace dizzying circles in the dust.
Father ponders the desert, the stars, the falling snow, the silence, the failed world—
these are, of course, the broad strokes (for the time to speak is short)—
and he understands that heaven's blank pages are uncountable, born of ash

like lamentations' shadows, like quarks rubbed to nothing by faith alone.
So Father's mind runs its scales: the Temple curtain wavers,
someone's left the Gate ajar, but the Kingdom remains dead still.
You cannot imagine how still. You cannot imagine that music.
In the chasm of God's gaze, the clamorous world readies its sacrifice.
You cannot imagine what these words lay bare, even in your final thought.

#19 (1/22/2022)

Hope's curious stalemate with the truth (a thing remembered only) turned
 to smoke.
Every blessed thing made visible was wrapped in a shroud.
From our red lives the embers flew up into shocked air.
We became enamored of a new firmament   a new darkness.
The tripwire of God's laughter triggered cataclysms.
The broken plow was pummeled by waves   so we took up new burdens
When the river turned to blood we drank wine.   We erased the atlases.
And then we began to see just what was your creation   your imagination
 made visible
like a set of teeth upon a silver plate   like a landmine in the garden
your kingdom of bright doors upon the unreachable summit
your old thirst set loose   your black ladders   your boulders and brambles.
Through you to us this world must pass   and there you will be named—
the binding quorum of absence our only promise in all matters
our words (these splintered crosses) mere shadows of the silence between us

#20 (1/23/2022)

The instructions were never quite right   never quite clear
Length   width   placement   distances arranged   suggestive shapes
I have come so far yet now after years I begin to question
Why are things on fire? Why is the December sun an unread book?
I came to you, thinking you knew the answer   but nothing lifted your gaze
your dreaming body an unknown language   and now I see
You have voyaged beyond my reach   the wind our falling makes the only
 thing that unites us
(our mutual horizon)   and I must watch the seasons pass and pass
each year another crest obscured behind the last   as paradise recedes
and the summer camp diversions   bright bodies on the beach   voices of
 loved ones
all of memory's flotation devices   approach their inevitable failure
sinking into darkness   while I   in my chosen craft   so enamored of
 absence
I   in my hard-won solitude   in my holiest place   knowing in my

  humdrum heart
what is to come can still proclaim "You have everything you wanted"

#21 (1/23/2022)

Waking from an unexpected sleep you try not to notice your actual life
small river flowing through the world of things the Thursday lawn work
the scheduled luncheons the "meetings after meetings" and the bark and slobber
of botched communication but despite your efforts some fragment of your attention
finds itself nameless and shaking gripping the wheel with both hands and thinking
"I'm here where I've always been This dark highway was always my destination
and these small struggles the angels I've invented to count myself blessed
now read to me from an empty book" You listen to that silence Your body bears
the strangling weight of all you loved in the world Soon your thoughts loosed
from the prayers and clumsy anthems that bound you loosed from the bells and lyres
loosed from the god whose name you thought you knew will sink into their last music
a dust dream more blank than you can comprehend quieter than heaven
But until then how loud it is your small river washing away the near bank
this stream of yours even if you don't know its name bearing you to anyplace but home

#22 (1/25/2022)

His eyes crack bluish mounds of ice Tuesday's voice is white, shifting
Remember small maps A Russian diplomat on a freight train wears a skinny tie
An old lady wrapped in cellophane carries pictures of death, but her book brings words
to sustain us The total is accurate I want them the way they are
I locate evidence in the mirror reminding me that I resemble myself less each year
A hole I can't identify swallows our names The dark insistence of her flesh carries
a formula for light so ban the use of named objects The air is full of language
If you roll a shadow around this word even the waves will speak

I keep talking golden chandeliers   my words depleted among the sluggish
        grays of the sea
In the monk's hard white room, pages of code remind us   pain lasts forever
I'm not certain I remember her face or the light of the curtains   but the dark
        mouth of desire
still consumes me   Its brittle wire suspends a painted bird with too many wings
The smothered flutes are becoming abstract   like someone else's thirst
He looks at his hunger in the glass   and understands that his absence is
        what is missing

#23 (1/26/2022)

In certain men skepticism is a knife to the throat   They pick up packages
        and make a list
of what is missing   approach the world by falling   take head counts in
        the dark
and suffer a distant look as night tips in   They do not believe that each dim
        image
supports a star   no   Everything is a dish of chemicals   a wheel of stone
In the mirror a half-evaporated face becomes a quern of doubt   and this
        little hole of self
with its hungry music   sees only the flaw for which it is looking   sees
        that the sky
is leaving   sees the identical days skid by   takes measurement of the
        wounds
the shadows of birds   the crumbling clouds   the impenetrable prose of
        the world it knows
it will have to erase   the dissolving fictions   the snag   the chain   the handles
        of meaning
no noon replaceable   no thirst blessed   and all the dreams are burning holes
This is the story of who I am   always forgetting the names   alone on my
        private gallows
my curiosity and pleasure dwindled to an aching tooth   a parachute of
        pain easing me
to the ground   I am thinking of tearing out my memory with a new language
        in which
it hurts to mean something   and with each star I name I'll hear the shattering
        of a world

#24 (1/28/2022)

The silent onlooker whose wet teeth and dry brain click in time reminds us
to worship the great verbs that bear our desire   In this Theater of Mirrors I find
my mistaken identity   amidst the stolen faces   the eyes congealed in silver

"The essential part is written down" shouts the drunken helmsman   I keep
          this covenant
stitched across my eyelids   Your absent bones shape the masonry of my
          thoughts
As more agile tongues fly toward heaven   mine is content to mold the moon
to watch the edge of my dream curl into flame   to watch the tidepool sparkling
          with gems
Whatever I sought to buy is bought   The door swings open   The great
          chamber
of blood and pain   of butterflies at the bottom of wells   awaits its guest
          its ghost
The indifferent fountains swell and burst   I suffer in vain   The mantle
          clock proclaims
its aphasia   The grimy window with its belly full of trees and light imagines
          rose gardens
only because night is coming   and there are gods waiting inside to get out
          They tack
manifestos to the walls of labyrinths   build cathedrals in the snow   construct
          constellations
using a grammar lost to us   who dwell beneath their metaphors in our dark
          houses

#25 (1/29/2022)

A swimmer in the froth of dreams wears a white mask as camouflage
In my gown of shadow, I see beneath all polyhedrons to the whirling eye of dust
Prayer wheels pulse with odd laments   Drowned prophets rise
The wind sings sonatas of crystal to the listening sea as the sky fills with
          angels bearing
skeleton keys and proclaiming the seven types of ambiguity   I am whipped
          by a lover's gaze
Meanwhile, night has eaten all the bridges   The intervals between nothing
          and nothing
go unmeasured by the metaphysical lecturers dragging their wounded kites
across the sand   My spent art and my chromatic fantasies unravel in your eyes
The alphabet ends not with ink and disquiet but with death's white writing
and the idiot posturing of bones   The reader can't find the one way out
From the pier's end I observe the horizon hemorrhaging with secret messages
I gather husks of words   the furious hymns of my inward moon   odes
          scrawled on cellophane
The seven mirrors tell me "You're on your own"   My hemophiliac clock
          bleeds hours
As the years spin and fall my compass turns into the stone I must swallow

#26 (1/31/2022)

I unbutton my nightmares until nothing remains but domestic anachronisms
Invisible louvers screen out the angels' white glare   My thoughts hide themselves
in tromp L'oeil effects and attacks of conscience   We look at one another meaningfully
My old friend says it's hard to hold back tears when the moon dispenses metal filings
on the man-made pond   This is what it means to feel your ragged brainwaves blossom
despite the paperweights   I could listen to that stranger's eyes all night   Did you find your
way around the gristmill to the onyx maze with its beautiful turnstile attendants?
Is there a word to end all words?   What is this liquid whisper inside the closet
but the abstract buzz of broken feelings or a cryptic alphabet recited by a saintly voice?
I am stirring all that passed between us into a stew of keyholes   I am looking across
the valley to your sixteen windmills and ruby umbrellas   I want to be your sleeve
Even now I hear the horn's blast and taste the thumbprint of your eyelashes
These false doors were put up for a reason   These accidents no longer appear random
Things we love to see appear to us in dreams just as the full moon secretes its marrow

#27 (2/11/2022)

Those years happened in China   Our clairvoyant whispers excused themselves, and
moon-broth filled the empty room the way stupid questions fill an unhappy childhood
In a cornfield a singing boy chased a saint   The Curator of Silhouettes rode a surrey
Into nameless lands   Vocabularies exploded   The sea's ad infinitum reassured
the abstract thinkers killing time in their glass houses   August outgrew us
Maybe we could throw in some different outcomes If we use a different catapult
Maybe we daydreamed the wrong vanishing points   the wrong gossamer angels
Someone said "No way of knowing something half-hidden"   there is no word
to end all words   we had so many that we didn't know what to do with them   truly it seemed

we lived between signals   so when two butterflies left skid-marks in the
         empty sky
it seemed to us the birth of a galaxy   and our heads filled with stars
Since then we've barely learned from our mistakes   Fifty years later all the
         maps unfurled
You learned to read with your eyes closed   I suspect the story is a good one
its drought-filled decades unraveling as love withdraws   taking our names
         with it

#28 (10/10/2022)

The day you tried to put things over   the strong sea lurked in my empty bed
I was glad   I sang   I hungered   and advanced upon complete nothing
my eyes jeweled   the vision fitted for glasses   a dream from the start
Jerked onward by love's rope   I mapped my way out and back
my mouth sewn shut   dying and absurd   moonless
I followed the great River through the green and forgiving wood
And in my brain nobody was missing   the relaxed lotus   sweet milk of home
Is this what's meant by "in the clear"?   On this threshold I come to make
         amends
the dark swerve of my famished youth a ground-rhythm the listener won't
         make out
as I feel or fail the blind song in my bones   Can we then walk into the sky
like a vanished thing taking hold   on pages barren and white
that place where nobody was   setting thought to time
looking out past snows and summers   sideways   at the growing dark
and say without one glorious sigh   "Thank you for everything"?

#29 (10/12/2022)

Against noon's vacuity   impenetrable   as clarity is impenetrable
or consciousness without object is impossible   the eye shipwrecked on
         the singular
motes in the air   a fly in a bottle   an old man glassed in a dream's frozen
         moonlight
Poetry is death's denial   though poets jostle each other and cannot defend
         their metaphysic
they feel the word's roots grip down   thin twigs into branches   into myth
         and covenant
at the mind's end   singing of the imaginable sea   of silence imagined as
         transparence
thickening the air   To see the people   "to visit other islands"   to speak
         of public justice
and make indifference crumble like the hard edge of concrete   to take the

        pulse of sorrows
and know it is the real that we confront   which may crack open
as sidewalks and minds are said to   and the weight of cause cannot
        explain itself
for these are the words we choke on   our art an isolation of the actual
        which is too little
too little the ghosts and glitter   too little the feathery serpent unfurling
in our confused calendars   too little what has happened to me   an old
        man singing in the sun
his mind rising   imagining itself rising   above the pipes and broken works
        of the world

#30 (10/14/2022)

Each day   black flamed   burns the past   Each night groans in your own voice
The new horizon is a naked sword   disemboweling the sea
The weird troubadour of Saint-Merry heard a flute dying
and abandoned all memories of childhood with its terrifying shades of blue
now he barks at lilacs and passes for a pimp on the rue de Verrerie
singing of monsters that dispel deep knowledge and leave abysses in their wake
as troupes of organ grinders patrol the border crossings in the poet's brain
where a white rose is singing   A tiny acrobat salutes us   We say goodbye
to the century of sawdust and little reed pipes   Shapely harmonium music
        none of us could bear
flows beneath a cloud made of eyes   I worship Zeno astride an invisible tree
My epitaphs run dry   The fatal word falls like a shooting star   all opulence
        and frothing mirage
Such pious bells!   A banquet of pale mouths ushers in the new epoch
Under his gas mask the grammarian waggles a dust-colored tongue
And the thorns of the wire have somehow grown more beautiful
Leaving me to count numberless silences   with the moon's pallor in my throat

#31 (10/15/2022)

Face down in poetry-schemes   awaiting the swoon of whispers
I feel these albatross sentences becoming ever more centrifugal
The words emerge   a new skin   forgotten etymologies   dream fulcrums
Irregular verbs drunk in cars   clouds of white numbers   and myths in
        sleep's clothing
Why this devotion to outcast echoes?   The passions of men come to nothing
The mirror's black holes   distance and time scraping at the glass
Bodies aching to remember love's missing pages   The original language is
        a map
of impermanence   the first metaphor a dead angel a priori

Chthonic deities practice sleight of hand in their dark towers   and each
    human skull's
a labyrinth of signs   Each stammering poem explodes perpetually into the
    uncreated
the fundamental silence   Each single word burns the incense of sun-spent
    eternity
What little we know is memory   a falling star   and nothing else will follow
So how was your summer?   Were we crazy-drunk and wrecked by music?
Did the symbols speak their pluralities?   Did we dare the thunder to erase
    our names?

Carnal Acoustics

1

contrary simplicity: natural born hammer-scribbler defangs theory under weight of swamp-pink dream-swoon

unchecked fuck-tizzy melts lace   leaves vestigial foretaste   as wet narcissism advances pocket trauma   closes the book on tenure

meanwhile horizontal showboats maze into punctual fissures   (forked tongue the result)

messianic Uber driver unmakes history   sleepyhead delirium slinking past monitors and vibratory lips

encrypt in residual fictions   gobbling floating mirrors and sincere floozies in vinyl attire

while between my legs blued corollaries gate-crash chaste enzymes with itchy dioramas and leaky choirboy vespers

no wonder I'm craving pimento   eroticized half-hitches and moons "torn from the headlines"

the humming surrender of untenable flesh like an irruption of Ann Bolelyns in high wattage heels

patronizingly seducing grammatical zippers by word of mouth and fashionable state-sponsored lexicons

2

blonde asterisks wake the Phrasemaker with twirly clamor   inveigle fat fallacies and mouth baubles

eroticized thrall-puddles detonate in brunette disguises   dissembling hat-box-juiced insurrection

romance peeper retro-fondles condominium-faced pouter   wanton swallower of votive tinsel

whose claustrophobic spandex elicits crevice-envy and self-reproach among gourmet submissives

as erstwhile language splurge throat-throttles economists who dream of golden means

combustible discharge   horsehead prototypes buttercup-lancing encore root

whispering in mojo gear   unmasking blushes   dusty lip attachments   intimate slow burn

"your bait is uninspired" (she said)   measured in jelly   truant   drowsy saddled with expression   ripe for closure

like infected bonbons afloat in the petri dish of your eyes   little sleeping mannikin chewing the orchids

3

melancholic angel curfews   linguistic bungee-snapping foreplay   seminary egg-sucker calibrates sugary martyrdoms

as pixilated crotch jockeys parachute into Pentecostal ballrooms   hankering for fisticuffs and confectionary lace

damp revenge fantasies   chlorinated brain froth   eyebrow-penciled diphthong-whackers screaming "sniff the hypotenuse, Nigel!"

wrecking crew bowknots random gonads   deriding epiglottises with nearly frozen oompahs

bifurcating hedgerow   gliss of adherence   junction box-swapping carbonated yawp upheaval

rounding third   butch hip   lingerie fizzes   pendulum-exquisite bliss device (sans corduroys)   bitch-slapped ala mode

as in "turnip of your mire"   as in "hot-lagged ovum fence wired for fraud and gutted idioms"

as in "dishonorable discharge":   lips moving when you read   stylized kisses meteor-showering honeyed atolls

between jack-knifings   he wore legato gloves to the clambake   slurped hormonal roux and who shall 'scape whipping?

4

pinkflamed eunuch halo reflect on the process   fallacious desiderata jittery with beelines

and nape fat arrestingly coddled   clock tease   red solicitors' binary hula hoop

thigh muffin   lenient green prom gown figure-eights amidst paint-by-numbers clown-faced tomfoolery

reap fixed stars   cajoling fragrant gravy from boyish tableaus   kamikaze turtle-wax

at least the night is young   and this vulnerability gel's tender know-how bullets sugarplums   (torso gloss notwithstanding)

while my surname in the crosshairs lives on in "personal memory" and zealous dream-screen silhouettes

spermicidically marshmallowing voids   thrust-gauge vowel-wetting enjambments espied from cupolas

the static roses and sexual pollen and grammatically valentining lyrics writ large on bus station bathroom mirrors

hoochie coochie paradiddle springs for woodcocks   credent ear or toy in blood   happily ever-aftering

5

another nocturnal cocktail spasm   Venus-fingered honey-warp surgically notched

her buttress flown   serving mouth subpoenas and willy-nillying Tuesday goosebumps paratactically

a clerical choke-collared nimrod flurry triggers omniscience   spittoon abysses symbolically deepen

heliotropic groin varnish downsy-daisying involuntary umlauts and monomaniacal fur-balls

dining on pudding fatale   self-impinging hump-flap   fallopian cunning and penis archetypes

pronoun prolapse va-va-vooms Mr. Mumbles   his borscht is a-cold   (poor Tom!)

storm on her heath   guzzle cherubs   moist sublimations in parking lot epiphanies

twist spree   lumpen promise   spank-lozenge   secret bubbles   categorical imperatives for sale or lease

lascivious somersaulting cream-adherent infinitival smack-dabber at your service Mum

6

remorseless carousel of vellicating nom de plumes   spoon-tongued interruptus

strip-searched in crawl-spaces   bleeding ever fixe'd   betrothed to stalemates intentionally fungal

the oceanic body's "temporal sfumato" like dream-kibble flotsam deflowered at intervals

"give it to me straight"   sex so syntactical   within reach-around of easiest Rorschach ink-splats

kiosk pheromones goose sales   fondled algorithms and market-erections rub lotion on my dialectic

I speak in papier-mache   and stay for coming attractions   O rubber lamb pliably lurid bisque-stained huffer

somewhat salty to the touch   anatomical sideways squeezes with falsetto nightsticks

tenderloin-gibbering   peristaltic   yodeling doxologies in 6/8 time   and always cleft for

Rabelaisian midriff target-shooters from whom all blessings flow in the thinnest of airs

7

Mr. Mumbles' *nachträglichkeit* in fishnet hose   Pavlov-soaked Beatrice-in-reverse   (still a banker's daughter)

hashtag #comes in handy   sips nacre unabashed to completion   pimping dial-up bliss and

membrane-caprice   frappe' du mal   serpent hissing algorithms   dragged down to second circle

wind-jerked tempest-tossed   contrapasso   Wi-Fi girls "just miles away"   expense of spirit waste of   keypad peep show   skip the ad in 3   2   1

boogie sauce cleanup in aisle seven   Catullan sparrow-fluff   40 percent off with approved credit

maladaptive orchids   kite tail pain salts the sky with moon detritus and wet mirror polarities

identical turnstiles   hip-flown flags   flute-junk gerrymanderers of desire no sooner proved

than despise'd straight   the marsh stench and stale wine aftertaste   lingering

8

palely loitering lyricist triggers talcums nightly   scores video penetration

rubs tandem signs on stilts   (dream rinse repeat)   girdle and honey jar

thigh-bone ram-scarred   credit check   pleasurable static   Circean luau charged to your account

rhetorical half-way houses' background music   soften for the kill

hypertrophic balloon sputum   gingerly jazzed analgesic embrace

"if you're happy, I'm happy"   black-lotused sex embezzler wishin' you were here

sans merci   keeping stiff upper lily-brow   "in language strange"

fever-dewed   eluded prick-praxis   flunitrazepam exchanged for "fragrant zones"

analogies eclipsed   metonymies shattered   just nerve-buzz in dendrites like bare trees where late the sweet birds sang

9

the locust in my groin   sings among assassins   sentimentalists in "surplice white"

sub-Platonic grifters bearing pornographic cuspidors   Teflon angels   gravy whips

wet martyrs (home-styled) suffering third degree dream-burns   cause Mr. Mumbles to shoot the bolt

make furtive cash withdrawals beneath new moons (reflected in a crow's left eye—hey-ho!)

summon plastic-spurred satyrs and vibrating kewpie dolls   self-marinating in "light enough to read by"

and in the end grown bitter in his darkening tower   treading undertows establishing radio silence

cyclops-eyed   vinegar-tongued   increasingly vestigial   with knock-kneed syntax and a host of word-borne viruses

mirror-mocked   nerve-bare   unfriended   no perch for his condescension defiantly writing apostrophes to no one

Time Curve Postlude

She said, "You should adjust your moon acumen."

       I said, "What does that mean?"

She said, "It's like a wishbone, only saltier."

       I said, "I still don't follow."

She said, "I've watched your clammy feelings distribute party favors, Gustave, and it excites me."

       I said, "Undress me in French, Belinda Souffle."

She said, "I will, but I have one question. I've noticed that you secrete stained glass at irregular intervals. Is that because you're a poet?"

As if on cue, I secreted a stained glass portrait of Saint Dwynwen of Wales.

       I said, "A poem is where the fingerprints show.
       Will you accompany me along this white boulevard?"

She took my arm, and together we walked, as rampant fog excommunicated the dust. We passed many a cul de sac along the way. At one, we observed a crowd of minimalists standing outside an arboretum, clutching their empty sketchpads.

She said, "Do you remember the day you lost your circumference in Sea Isle City? We were strolling along the beach, and you said something about Time Curves. What was it?"

       "When time curves, things repeat."

"That's it. When time curves, things repeat. And the moment you said it, all the calendars turned their blue keys. We could hear the tumblers yielding with a universal groan. Then we tried to hold a mirror up to all our past mistakes, hoping by doing so to render them commercial-free, but to no avail."

       "No avail."

"And that's when you lost your circumference to the Venus-foam of Sea Isle City," she said.

"I remember," I said.

At that moment, a trumpet tantara rent the sky. I wanted to curl up inside her interstices and practice Dorian scales. I wanted to travel the length of her tropes, as if through a wormhole. I wanted to be her adjoint operator, to ravish her wishbone along a complex matrix in Hilbert space, to wax her transom and whisper schwas in her one good ear.

> I cried, "Tell me, Belinda Souffle, with your ampersand hair, your dress made of crossword puzzles, and your eyes awash with algorithms, what would it take to drain the moon acumen from your lips?"

She said, "Each word, each sentence, lures us into a cul de sac of its own making. But sometimes the words come unmoored, their orbit more entropic and their echoes fainter, like church bells heard underwater, or the voice of a dream-narrator remembered suddenly in the tepid light of day. Every poem is a collapsing wave function, Gustave. They clatter about us like a hail of moon cartilage, then sink into the empty page. Perhaps even this one."

> I said, "Pray for us, Saint Dwynwen, in the hour of our paraphrasable longing." Then I said, "Tell me, Belinda Souffle, how is it after all these years, you are still my watershed—and your memory my paperweight? Why is your every touch like spooky action at a distance? Why must we go on gathering corn-cockle and picking up stray gloves along the Rue Fontaine? Why must we paint childhood landscapes using three shades of white?"

Belinda Souffle flashed a translucent smile. "Because moon acumen is a tale told by the winners," she said. "Because downward spirals come in threes. Because most utopias prove unwieldy, and only through a leap and a turning can the unfamiliar be glimpsed. Because you can't paraphrase a poem without thumbscrews. Because you lack a circumference, Gustave, and the reason for that is that you lack a center. But mostly," she said, as the great wave rose behind her, towering higher and higher until it blocked the sky, "because we'll never be commercial-free, no matter how many mirrors we hold up to our mistakes. Do you understand what I'm saying, Gustave? Please tell me you understand."

> "I'm beginning to," I said, reaching out an imaginary hand to touch her cheek—but by then it was already too late, because the water covered everything.

Furthermore

Orchids sleeping in closure
burn attachments

    Unmask golden memes:
    brunette insurrection
    detonates mouth submission

Lexicons and grammatical heels
untenable pimento

    Moon vespers ululate
    enzymes leak from vinyl lips
    pink swoon theory/wake the clamor

Fondle wanton tinsel
jerry-rigging seminary martyrdoms
penciled and chlorinated oompah-gliss
replaces "lingerie mode" wired for honeyed idioms
the "sugary parachute"

    Carbon-copied neuropathic process
    binary prom tomfoolery coddle bedstraw bellflower
    figure-eights in "personal memory"

Metonymic mind-sprawl crosshair silhouette
clown-faced turtle wax
reap boyish gravy (such know-how notwithstanding)
vowel-wetting seen from cupolas
notched spasm serving moths

    Surgically varnished umlauts
    Paratactical Tuesday promise-lumps
    deepen spittoon matrix

Crawl-spaces, intentionally fungal (flotsam at intervals)
nightstick interruptus trumps Rorschach bisque blot
cherub lunch "special sale or lease" bubble fallopian epiphanies
dial-up frappe' yodeling thinnest of intervals

Second circle aftertaste fluff
approved credit membrane linger
talcum penetration nocturnal jar

Luau sputum/lily dream
flunitrazepam among sentimentalists
left eye radio silence surplus Teflon
defiantly self-marinating vinegar host (natural born)

     encrypt pink trauma   unmake tenure
     between my legs   residual fiction
     punctual floozy foretaste   state-sponsored craving
     mojo corduroys   pout horizontal
     monomaniacal bowknot   squeeze tenderloins

Degenerates your refusal factory cupcake avarice licks commodities talking forever acoustic soup—salt hammer Wall Street shark cage, no extension cord. Have you eaten? TV exhaust pipes bee-line into brain stem—got it? Vinyl hem-length accommodates balance sheets. Besmirched silence. Corybantic mule-skinners gate crash the diaphanous. Snowflakes, bells: incantations on paper, "poetry-as-conformist-entertainment." Verbal kenosis.

     the usual lisp
     childhood parentheses
     text of beauty marks
     and blue flame

Freely admit penny-whistle salesmen, bird whisperers, self-Ouija-ing nominalists stuck in syntactical flypaper. Little tugboat doo-dahs make it numb. Deep red codex. Acapella stomach protractors. "Hoping things will turn around." Basement full of category mistakes, septic chum, and so I ask you: did I pay too much for your ontology? Smell of cufflinks, fractal dreams. What you call "pushing" I call "helping." Someone defamiliarized the ice trays—left quadrant frisson an early symptom, mirror numbness in later stages. You suck ammo. Sleepy Germans come undone remembering moon-mist and sincere lakes from childhood. That's why you should never hand an amnesiac a plumb-line! Gray hum beneath the lyricist's prattle—that's the ticket!

a new prose born of lyric enervation
watching shadows recoil from "realistic moons"
emerge from folds or creases darker than the mirror's back
a word's torn wing or whitening echo
Schoenberg sonatas   flapjack boys   the body's forgetful solarium now tenebrous poems
(aren't they all?)   ay-ay sir   community outreach "dialed up to ten"   a

gaggle of beatnik

marketeers ponder their reflections in department store display windows
and recuperative looking glasses   "fighting capitalism from within"
sentences grown more centrifugal   dreamed into substance
call it "music without metaphors   an alphabet of bones"   each name's
weightless embrace flat like throttled French phrases in a haughty maître d's
throat   foxhole amor   laryngeal croutons   fricative dispensary
functional butter fossilizes Protestant jerk emetic as forklift floozies seem
inherent   viral earworm discounted   corporate wham-bam   tiny
minotaur adrift on whimsical spreadsheets reminding us to dot bottom
lines   buckle up and knuckle down   (is there an acronym for
that?)   do you hear what's in the air—scale of one to twenty-six?
predictable moon-light falls aslant upon my "unreadable text"
good fog
fricative fricative   harsh your mellow   feeling interpolated?   a pain is
a pain   is pain

"all I do is bleed"
salt savory
arguable thesis

a long line of guttersnipes
lollygagging Sartrean schmerz-fest!
what is there to interpret?
are you wordsome tonight?

>   what I meant to say, O imaginary lover, is "diddle-yum this, *a priori*!"
>   The rest is silence.
>   Furthermore . . .

Tapioca Verdigris

sado-lyrical   theory-scented   self-troweling   *fleur de lis*-adjacent
null-spurting   sieve-lipped   reverse-mimetic   ear-jerked
spool-kissing   post-amniotic   meme-grubbing   scuttle-tongued
hydro-coiffed   pseudo-phobic   anal-inventive   smudge-friendly
retro-Hegelian   clitoral-remiss   poon-befuddled   lisp-hording
narco-omniscient   aspic-induced   Ur-tumescent   bonbon-fitted
psycho-linguistic   near-fetched   *d'etre*-scented

(Enter the narrator with a diabolical pompadour. He speaks.)

"Keep the observer out of the description,
    for as we know
        what roses remain
            have nothing left to do
                with toothless frostweed's bitter love."

proven insufficient   now absorbing lubricants
supine with synecdoche
random iotas   culpable pie

"Would someone vulcanize my forte, 'ere the magpies billow?'"

(The narrator seems to be proposing a "false consciousness reach-around" in a two car garage)

"Withdraw upon your melancholy wings.
    Ignore the distinctive crybaby haunting of
               red ghosts drinking names
through incisions in memory."

anecdotal lipstick   gulping fall guy
    verb-mitered   damp impertinence
        diagnosis retro-fitted elastic horn-rimmed nostalgia
or maiden voyage torso laminator steeped in god terms
            fluent lozenge guzzler incubate ennui
homunculus flambe' sheathed in falsehoods   her nest feathered
            astride carousel daydreams
        thrice-bestirred goo clinic
      bullfrog praxis Thermador infarction
  fuse latent   homecoming downwards

                    bullet point follicle cream interloper
                                        dollar signs for eyes
kidney-limping ecclesiastical puff   matrilineal
              signifying urchin nodes
                        Sadie Hawkins freeze frame sobriety check
                                                                her
                    faux touch knee bends up
          (faun may dread real arrows)
dazed myth   brain-slaughter
                                seaside spa   "spite-lickings"

(The narrator sings with lute accompaniment.)

"O she's a pheromoaner
a regret-bubble saboteur
a permeable self-box laminator
refusing pillow talk"

(He pauses, dreamy-eyed, awaits applause that never comes. Then he points a finger directly at the reader.)

"Though I be mantis-eyed and aberrant, these tithe-sniffers I'll no longer abide!
Uncoddled flux redeemer, pivot now!
(Why does this broth taste disdainful?)
Don't you know the rose has withered? Don't you know
          December frostweed
                    forms ice flowers
                              replacing summer blooms?"

the stuttering nights   *too late*   the sexual filibustering moon pouring talcum in the wine   *too late*   the séance-audits and amnesiac nuptial swooning   the regretful nacre in silver thimbles   the slipknot orthodoxy and commodified pangs   *too late   too late*   the lacquered sincerity and practiced "catch" in the voice   the entropic similes crooned over car radios   the fatalism by candlelight   the lilac whips   the Keatsian sigh the hormonal eclipse and emotional neap tide with its swash zone of dream rinds and lost car keys   *too late   too late   too late*

(The narrator wishes to distract you with rhetorical flagellation.)
(Isn't that what you wanted? Isn't that why you came?)

"Existential peepshow flunky with your Lenten stalagmite fantasies, cease
          your arrhythmia!
Quell your dipodal longings. Cast aside your lyrical pining.
     Fetch me some squid-finesse!
          Sniff intimate fractals.

These wanton lacunae on freckled mattresses were my idea...
as was
THE TAPIOCA VERDIGRIS!"

cramp-flavored   candy-itching   mire-infused   rhizome-smitten
strangler-ready   Naugahyde-friendly   vibro-fellatial
congenitally-rose-malingering   micro-Platonic   inter-axial
hanky-turvy   kiss-proof   faery-orbed   counter-truculent
margarine-besmirched   omni-distant   porridge-begetting
quasi-orgasmic   auto-phallic   Uber mensch-besotted
trans-gelatinous   infra-Pentecostal   hyper-mammalian
toadying-soft-palette-logjam-gobbing   proto-spasm

(The narrator raises an eyebrow and offers the reader a spoon.)

Stop Charging Us Money To Watch You Sleep

the true grounds of any ratiocination * mere substitutive systems * open-mouthed over a harmonium * the deep focus, the long takes * the "moon" emptied of eye-sockets * replacement of belief by feeling * that tinkling sound of similar endings * mouthed tinsel sentiment

played out under your lids   "our job as models is to sell"
take dictation with a scalpel   habitual word-use renders unseen
meaning as "determinate absence"   machine that drives the poem's con-
ception

I observe that the place is nearly empty—and the wrong color, albeit one possessing "an incredible clarity."
(Her yellow scarf shimmered with the "approved" nuance.)
Now do continue.
Our feelings are strictly decorative.
My brain makes whimpering noises, polishes bannisters in the dark.
Were you thankful when the silver birds turned translucent?
Did we make obtuse catcalls on love's fractal shore?
These are, of course, the wrong questions.
Let's slide back into "the human range," with its thin substratum of irony.
Clearly, our fashionable days are coming to an end.

chained to flickering shadows/ TV screen as cave wall/ drama coaches/ routine surveillance/ knowledge confused with hormonal secretions/ shiny images replacing printed words/ junk politics/ image-based cultures/ communicating through narrative, pictures, pseudo-drama/

                 O lyrical "deleveraging"!
         O lyrical "structural investment vehicles"!
              O lyrical "credit default"!
             O lyrical "securitization"!

"My voice sounds different in print."   *as if thistles*
"Is it possible to exist outside of description and narration?"   *of pearls*
                                                           the white gesture
"Coherence seems an error of the senses."   *agreement-pimping digit*
"What's your cover story?"   *i.e., a.k.a. "shimmering calyx"*
"Forgetting offsets perception."   *property of transparence*
"Find the statements you cling to and ask yourself why." *like fleeting thrones*

"What I want to know is, are the
'artistic features' of a text intrinsic to it,
or are they defined by 'institutional
conventions?' Ditto for these feelings."

> *Rain plied the lovers with its silver needles, its cold exclamation points.*
> *It made a sound like plangent harpsichords, etc.*

"We started out toward a condition of meaningfulness, characterized by
borrowed statues and gilded marionettes, but soon we realized that
the political implications of our mental puppetry
were 'indistinguishable from the emotional truths.'"

(Remember, the prop man hasn't always read the script.)

What is the Ur-word for "tremulous veil"?
    "We didn't invent the language."
        To write is to summon dead voices.
            Heigho! The wind and the rain.

> *Even then, as we slow-danced,*
> *I understood that the paint-by-number*
> *clown portraits on her basement wall*
> ***symbolized** something.*

But enough mimesis.

(Yesterday the prop man served notice: we were running out of attic space and other aporias. "It's all those old mannequins," he said. "They keep piling up. Maybe we should donate a few to Goodwill before they commence narrating personal memories?")

Do you seek *le mot au jus*?
Has the biopsy found evidence of manufactured tears?
Does all writing tend to its horizon?
Have you invented terms of nostalgia the advertisers can use?
Have you indulged in the capacious category of charms?
Why are memories said to spring from wounds?
Does coherence offer itself as "proof of truth"?
Are your bizarre turns of language the products of a torturous state of mind?
Has your sudden insight been followed by philosophical maxims?
Have you restated your desire in less ambiguous terms?
Will your accumulated references enthrall the reader?
Has interpretation been limited by imposition of an ever-more specific context?

O lyrical "commodity fetish"
O lyrical "stylized acquiescence"!
O lyrical "cottage industry"!
O lyrical "codification of the serialized individual"!

A man with a slogan has no need for narrative   *as weeping stems from*
myopic amours
I slept through that story   *an old man's jar of train whistles*
She said, "We live in explanatory notes"   *a.k.a. "chewing the daffodils"*
Let's market this "clever derangement"   *her hand stirring tepid water*

"Welcome to the heart industry!" she said. "We've determined that your feelings are genuine."
Now the dumbwaiter in my chest may bear its tender cargo deep into the gloaming, trailing paper streamers in its wake.
Let each poem come with an imaginary stethoscope.
Let each tender iamb throb with significance.
I'd tell you more, but I left my comb and wax paper on the operating table.

"an object purified from all accidental moods" * self as series of "subject-statements" and/or caramelized slip-knots of feeling * blind moons and dream detritus * manipulating verb tenses for "reflection" * vertical axis pole-dance * call coming from "inside the house"

(When the prop man slips out back for a smoke, all the mannequins begin to chant in unison: "Gentle reader, let us tell you how we suffered for love.")

Grateful acknowledgment is made to the editors of the following journals:

AZURE: "The Mune Monologues"
The Decadent Review: "Furthermore" and "Tapioca Verdigris"
Lotus Eaters: "Effulgence at Three O'Clock"
Doubly Mad: "Oof!" and "The Arena"

Portions of "Carnal Acoustics" appeared in *SurVision, Clockwise Cat,* and *Doubly Mad.*

About the Author:

Thomas Townsley grew up in Central Pennsylvania. He earned his Master's Degree in English and Creative Writing at Syracuse University in 1983. These days, he teaches at Mohawk Valley Community College and spends ordinary evenings in New Hartford, NY "mining the marvelous" and practicing blues harmonica. His work has appeared in numerous journals and international anthologies of surrealist poetry. *Alphabet Noise* is his sixth book.